The GIRLS' BOOK of SECRETS

Shhh... Don't Tell!

Written by Gemma Reece
Illustrated by Katy Jackson
Edited by Hannah Cohen
Designed by Zoe Quayle

The GIRLS' BOOK of SECRETS

Shhh... Don't Tell!

Buster Books

First published in Great Britain in 2009 as a hardback called *The Girls' Book of Secrets*
by Buster Books, an imprint of Michael O'Mara Books Limited.
9 Lion Yard, Tremadoc Road, London SW4 7NQ
This paperback edition first published 2011.

www.mombooks.com/busterbooks

Text and illustrations copyright © Buster Books 2009
Cover designed by Angie Allison (from an original design by www.blacksheep-uk.com)
Cover illustration: Paul Moran

A CIP catalogue record for this book is available from the British Library.

ISBN: 978-1-907151-93-4

2 4 6 8 10 9 7 5 3 1

Printed and bound in May 2011 by Clays Limited, St Ives plc,
Popson Street, Bungay, Suffolk, NR35 1ED, UK.

Papers used by Michael O'Mara Books are natural, recyclable products
made from wood grown in sustainable forests. The manufacturing processes
conform to the environmental regulations of the country of origin.

NOTE TO READERS

The publisher and author disclaim any liability for accidents or injuries that may occur as a result of the information given in this book. Be particularly careful with scissors, needles, kitchen equipment, and hot liquids. Always get permission from an adult before using any tools or utensils. Be mindful of the ingredients listed and your own allergies and medical conditions.

Follow safety precautions and advice from responsible adults. Always wear appropriate safety gear, stay within the law and local rules, and be considerate of other people. Most importantly, use your common sense at all times. particularly when heat or sharp objects are involved.

CONTENTS

HOW TO KEEP A SECRET

It is very important to be able to keep a secret. The better you are at keeping secrets, the more your friends will trust you, and the more they will share with you. If you always blab, you might find that your friends won't want to confide in you any more. To be the best at keeping secrets, follow these rules.

WHY IS IT A SECRET?

Try to understand the importance of the secret you are keeping and why it must stay a secret. Think about how the person who has confided in you would feel if her secret got out around school. Put yourself in her position and imagine how you would feel if everybody knew your secrets.

DIARY DANGER

Writing your secrets down can help stop the urge to say them out loud. However, if you do write your secrets down in a diary, then you will need to make sure you hide the diary in a really safe place, far away from snooping eyes (see page 33 for some top-secret hiding places for a diary).

I KNOW SOMETHING YOU DON'T KNOW

Never say, 'I know something, but I can't tell you what it is.' Your friends will try all manner of tricks to get information out of you. If you fall into this trap, simply change the subject completely and hope your friends get bored with begging.

GOSSIP GUILT

Have you ever let a secret slip and then felt truly terrible immediately afterwards? Once you have blabbed you can't take it back and the damage is done. Remind yourself of this stomach-sinking feeling next time you get the urge to tell someone your secret and your mouth will magically stay shut!

BEWARE OF THE ENEMY

There is an old saying that goes 'Loose lips sink ships'. This wartime rhyme was designed to stop people blabbing secret information that could then be used by the enemy in battle against them. Say this rhyme three times in your head next time you are tempted to spill the beans and avoid giving any information away.

TELL NO ONE

Keeping a secret means that you tell absolutely no one – not your mum or your sister, not even your best friend. If a secret is just too big to keep to yourself, you could always try telling it to your cat or dog ... but be sure to whisper!

HOW TO MAKE A DESIGNER DIARY

A secret diary should be a thing of beauty that you treasure picking up and writing in. Follow the steps below to make your very own 'designer diary' to write all your secrets in.

You Will Need:

• a spiral-bound notebook (A5 size or smaller) • PVA glue • card • a sheet of wadding or foam • newspaper • a piece of fabric in your favourite colour (make sure the fabric is not see-through) • two lengths of ribbon (each roughly 50 cm long) • ruler • scissors • a variety of sequins, beads, buttons and gold and silver stars

1. Measure the height and width of the front of your notebook with the ruler. Use these measurements to cut out two pieces of card that are the same size.

2. Cover one piece of card in glue and stick it on to the sheet of foam or wadding. Using the edge of the card as a guide, cut away the excess foam or wadding.

Do exactly the same with the other piece of card.

3. Cut out two squares of fabric – each piece of fabric should be about 5 cm larger than the size of each piece of card around each edge.

4. Lay down some newspaper to avoid getting glue on your work surface. Next, cover the back of one square of fabric with plenty of glue. Place the padded side of one of the card pieces in the centre of the fabric square. Press it down firmly to make it stick.

Do exactly the same with the other piece of fabric and card.

5. Cut the fabric diagonally at the four corners of each piece of card, as shown here. Then simply fold that fabric over the sides of the wadding and use more glue to stick the edges down on to the card.

6. Now cover the front of your notebook with plenty of glue. Place one length of ribbon across it so that enough hangs over the edge for you to tie your diary shut.

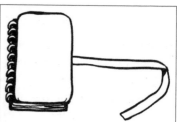

7. Stick one of the pieces of covered card over the ribbon on to the gluey surface of your notebook. Press it down firmly.

Now do exactly the same thing with the back cover of your notebook, adding a piece of ribbon in the same way and covering it with the other piece of card.

8. Leave your diary overnight to allow the glue to dry completely.

9. When the glue on your diary is completely dry, create a pattern of gold and silver stars, sequins and beads on the front and back of your diary. When you are happy with your design, stick each one down with a dab of glue.

10. Tie the two pieces of ribbon in a beautiful bow to hold your diary shut. Finally, sew a row of six buttons down the side of your diary. Sewing buttons to the fabric not only looks good, but will also help you create a code system, to ensure your diary remains unread (see opposite to create your own colour-code lock).

A COLOUR-CODE LOCK

Fixing a padlock to your diary will stop people from picking it up and reading it – but what if somebody gets hold of the key? With the key to your diary, someone could read all about your secrets, without you even knowing.

An effective way of securing your privacy is simply to create a colour code. Here's how you do it:

1. Find five large elastic bands – large hairbands would also work. You will need two of one colour, two of another colour and one that is a different colour from all the others.

2. Carefully wrap the elastic bands around your diary, positioning each band between the buttons that are sewn down the side of your diary. Arrange them in a special order that only you know. Here's one you could try:

Wrap two green bands at the top.
One yellow band in the middle.
Two blue bands at the bottom.

If the next time you pick up your diary the elastic bands are in the wrong order, you'll know instantly that someone has been snooping in your diary.

HOW TO DEVELOP SECRET HANDSHAKES

A cool way of greeting a friend when you meet up is with your very own secret handshake that only the two of you can perform. Here are a few that you could try. Once you've mastered these, you can have fun inventing your own top-secret handshakes.

BEST BUDDIES

SLIP 'N' SLIDE

WHAT'S UP

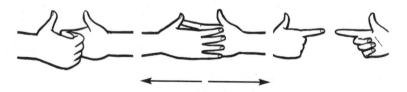

THE SECRET TO BEING CONFIDENT

Confident girls aren't born with bags of confidence – they have discovered the key to believing in themselves. Here are five confidence-boosting secrets.

Secret One – Stand Out. Don't be afraid to be different. Wear clothes you feel comfortable in that make you stand out from the crowd. Confident girls know that misfits rule the school!

Secret Two – Hold Your Head Up High. Don't slouch or slump. Instead, walk tall and proud – people will take notice of you. Make eye contact with everyone and strut your stuff like the confident diva you are.

Secret Three – Find True Friends. Find friends who understand you and like you for who you are. If your friends believe in you, you'll begin to believe in you, too!

Secret Four – Be Honest. It's difficult to be confident when you're pretending to be something you're not. Tell the truth at all times and be confident that being you is good enough.

Secret Five – Smile. Even if you aren't feeling smiley, smile and you'll immediately ooze confidence.

THE SECRET TO WEARING INVISIBLE MAKE-UP

Who needs make-up when you know the secret to looking beautiful without it? These sneaky beauty tips are especially good if you are not allowed to wear make-up to school.

The Perfect Pout. For luscious lips, brush a toothbrush gently across your lips to remove any rough skin. Finish off with a layer of lip balm.

Beautifying Brows. Frame your face by giving your brows a tidy. Stroke the hairs of your eyebrows upwards with a toothbrush. A tiny dab of petroleum jelly smoothed across the brows will set them in place.

Eye, Eye. Tired eyes? Pop two metal teaspoons in the fridge for half an hour. Place the round part of each spoon onto each of your eyes. The cool sensation will tighten the skin around your eyes, making you look bright-eyed and wide awake.

Get Cheeky.
Take the fleshiest part of your cheek between your finger and thumb and pinch lightly a few times to achieve a rosy glow.

HOW TO WRITE IN CODE

Writing in code is an excellent way to keep your secrets safe, or to communicate with your friends. Here are some codes to get you started. Once you've cracked these, why not invent some of your own?

CREATE CODE NAMES

If you are writing about somebody in your diary, why not use a code name for them? Write a 'key' on a piece of paper so that you can remember the new names that you give people, such as Becky = Sam, Mike = Alex. Memorise your key and keep it somewhere safe. Why not make a false-bottomed box (see how on page 59) for the perfect hiding place for your secret key?

Top Tip. Only use ordinary-sounding names – names such as 'Percival' or 'Ermintrude' will automatically arouse suspicion.

THE GRIDLOCK CODE

Begin writing your message in the bottom right-hand corner of a box-shaped grid. The letters of each word should run up and down the grid, from right to left, starting from the bottom end and moving up, as shown. Confuse the cleverest of decoders by inserting either an S, X, Y or Z, at the beginning and end of every new word.

X	E	S	Z	X
K	H	E	T	T
R	T	E	A	E
A	X	R	Y	E
P	N	H	E	M
Y	I	T	M	Y

Can you work out the message hidden in this grid?

Translation: Meet me at three in the park.

THE ALPHABET CODE

Write out the alphabet. Label each letter, from 1 to 26, like this:

A = 1, B = 2, C = 3, D = 4, E = 5, F = 6, G = 7, H = 8, I = 9,
J = 10, K = 11, L = 12, M = 13, N = 14, O = 15, P = 16, Q = 17,
R = 18, S = 19, T = 20, U = 21, V = 22, W = 23, X = 24,
Y = 25, Z = 26.

When you are writing in your diary, disguise important words by writing them in this code. For example:

When you are 23, 18, 9, 20, 9, 14, 7 in your 4, 9, 1, 18, 25, use this 3, 15, 4, 5.

Translation: When you are writing in your diary, use this code.

THE JUMBLE JIGSAW

Simply scramble up the letters of each word of your message to make a sentence that appears to be utter nonsense. The receiver of your coded message will have to unjumble each word, letter by letter, to discover its secret meaning. For example:

Oyu rea devtlni ot a cseert rvepoeles.

Translation: You are invited to a secret sleepover.

SECRET SYMBOLS

Draw some simple shapes on a piece of paper. Next to each shape write down the word that this shape will replace in your message. This is your secret key. Pass it around to your friends and agree only to write messages to each other using these symbols.

18

HOW TO WRITE A SECRET DIARY

Keeping a secret diary enables you to write down your innermost thoughts and wishes. However, if you find yourself staring at a blank page with a serious case of 'writer's block', here are some ideas to get you started.

Diary Dilemma. Decide what type of diary you are going to write. If you want to keep a straightforward journal, simply write down all the interesting things that happen to you each day and what you thought about each event.

List It. Alternatively, fill your diary with lists, such as a list of your best friends, a list of New Year's resolutions, of boys that you like (or don't like) and of bands that you love or hate. It will be fun to look back in years to come and see how your tastes have changed.

Set Targets. If your diary has a section for each day of the year, write messages on future days, such as 'Have you asked Mum about your sleepover yet?' or 'Have you learnt how to play guitar yet?' Draw a small box next to each question. When you get to that page, tick the box if you have achieved the goal described. If you have failed, re-enter it as a future goal.

Rate Each Day. Buy some stickers – small gold or silver stars are good – and give each day a rating. For example, a brilliant Saturday where you went ice skating and had an amazing chocolate milkshake would get five stickers, but a rainy Wednesday, with extra geography homework to do would get none.

THE SECRET TO COPING WITH HOMESICKNESS

Does being away from home make you want to curl up under a blanket and sob? Here's the inside story on how to cope when your pals, parents, and your own bed seem very far away.

FAMILY FEELINGS

Before setting off on holiday, select some photos of your family and friends and pop them in your suitcase. When you get to your destination, display them beside your bed. If you really miss your folks in the night, simply roll over to see their happy, smiling faces beaming down at you.

Remember, it is easy to phone, write to or email your family when you need them. Why not decide on a set time of day to contact your parents? You can focus on this during any wobbly moments.

BANISH THE BLUES

Fill your mind with positive thoughts. Instead of thinking, 'If I was at home, I could be cuddled up on the sofa watching a DVD with my sister,' tell yourself, 'I can watch a DVD any time. Today I will do something new and exciting.'

Remind yourself that you are only away from home temporarily. When you get back, your bedroom, house and family will still be there. You should try to make the most of the changes to your routine that a holiday offers. To stay positive, write down the new experiences you are having in your diary. List at least three interesting things that happen to you each day. Adventures never happen to those who fear leaving the comfort of their own homes. Once you're back home and your mum is nagging you to tidy your room, you might just wish you could go away again!

PLAN AHEAD

Perhaps when you are blue, what you are really feeling is disappointment with your holiday. Maybe you have been looking forward to going away for ages, but are not having as much fun as you had hoped. You might confuse the empty feeling with homesickness. Make sure you plan something fun to do right away. It is important to change how you feel about your holiday while you can still enjoy it.

SHARE YOUR FEELINGS

If you really can't help missing the people back home, don't bottle up your feelings. Confide in someone. One of your friends might confess that they often feel homesick, too.

HOW TO TELL IF SOMEONE HAS BEEN IN YOUR ROOM

Your bedroom is a great place to store your secret diary and to have your own private space. But how do you know if trespassers are snooping around when you're not there? Here are a few techniques you could try to catch out any sneaky snoopers – some are used by real spies.

PAPER TRAIL

Arrange some papers on your desk. Write the words 'TOP SECRET' on them. Using a ruler, measure exactly how much paper is sticking out from underneath each sheet of paper. Record these measurements. Leave your room for a few hours. When you get back, measure the distances between each sheet of paper again. If they've changed, you'll know that someone has been rifling through your papers without your permission.

POWDERY PRINTS

Sprinkle a small amount of talcum powder on the carpet by the doorway to your room. Only sprinkle a light covering – you don't want your parents to get suspicious about your spying techniques. When you return to your room, check the floor. If someone has been in, you'll see that the powder has been slightly trodden into the carpet.

Top Tip. Check for traces of powder on each member of your family's shoes. This may help you to identify your trespasser.

BALANCING ACT

Cut out a small slip of paper, roughly 1 cm by 2 cm. Open your bedroom door. Carefully climb onto a chair and place the piece of paper on the top edge of the door (be careful not to disturb the paper as you get off the chair). If someone does come in while you are out, you'll find the paper lying on the floor when you get back.

MOVEMENT DETECTORS

Cut some long, fine strips of paper – the finer the better as you don't want the intruder to detect them. Carefully insert the ends of each strip between the drawers of your chest of drawers. Gently close the drawers on them, leaving the tips of the strips hanging down.

If the drawers are opened while you are out, the movement will cause the strips of paper to fall onto the ground or into the drawers, alerting you that a snooper has paid an unauthorised visit to your bedroom.

HOW TO REVEAL THE SECRETS OF YOUR DREAMS

Many people believe dreams can reveal the secrets of your innermost feelings about your life and the people around you. Certain places or objects appearing in a dream can signify different things. Read on to find out how to record your dreams and discover their secret meanings.

KEEP A DREAM DIARY

Keep a notebook and pen beside your bed so that you can write down what you remember of your dreams as soon as you wake up.

DREAM ANALYSIS

Here's a guide to some common dreams, and what they may mean.

Eating An Apple. The apple symbolises the 'fruits of your efforts'. If you are eating and enjoying the apple, it can mean that you feel all your hard work has been rewarded.

Teeth Falling Out. This dream indicates you are worried about something or anxious about an embarrassing situation.

Flying. If you are able to fly during a dream, it shows you feel on top of a situation and have everything under control. However, if you suddenly can't fly when you think you can, it signifies doubts that you can maintain control of your life.

The Ocean. An ocean represents some difficulty in your life

that you are finding hard to overcome – you are feeling 'out of your depth'.

Being Chased. Dreams about being pursued often occur if you are experiencing a period of change in your life, and you are worried about failing new challenges.

Naked In Front Of The Class. This shows you are feeling vulnerable. You might also be feeling guilty or ashamed about something you've done, and afraid of being found out!

Pencil Breaking In An Exam. This reveals that you feel unprepared for a challenge that you are facing and are worried that people may expect too much from you.

Digging For Treasure. This often suggests that you are searching for something to make you happy and fulfilled in life.

HOW TO MAKE A COLOUR CODE

Use colours to create a code that will transmit secret messages to your friends. Below are a few colours and their meanings.

	TRADITIONAL MEANING:
RED	Red suggests extremes of emotion, either love or hate.
BLUE	Blue is associated with peace and tranquillity.
YELLOW	Yellow is used to cheer people up.
GREEN	Green brings good luck.
WHITE	White is associated with success and winning. It can also suggest secrecy.
PINK	Pink suggests beauty and extravagance.

Some colours have a traditional meaning and are associated with certain emotions. But now it's time to give them a new secret meaning that only your friends will know how to interpret.

COLOUR CODE:

Give a red present if you want to be best friends forever. Wearing a red hairband means you are angry with someone, but wearing a red bracelet shows you have a new secret crush.

Give a blue present if you feel relaxed in someone's company. Wearing anything blue on your top half (a scarf, T-shirt or cardigan) means 'I am sorry'. Wearing anything blue on your bottom half (tights, skirt, trousers or shoes) means 'I forgive you'.

Give a yellow present if someone makes you happy and you have a good giggle together. Everyone in your group or club should wear one item of yellow clothing on the day of a meeting, party or trip to show that you all belong together.

Give a green present to say 'I am lucky to be your friend'. Wear something green where it can't be seen to ensure really good luck, for example, you could wear a green vest under your T-shirt or a green pair of socks.

Give a white present if you trust someone completely. Tying a white ribbon to your bag or around your wrist means you have a secret. Wearing a white T-shirt on the day of a big match or competition will bring your team the top prize.

Give a pink present if you think someone is incredibly beautiful on the inside, as well as on the out. Wearing two plaits secured with two pink hairbands means you are calling an emergency secret sleepover to pamper and beautify your pals.

HOW TO MAKE FORTUNE COOKIES

A fortune cookie is a sweet biscuit that is normally served at the end of a meal in Chinese restaurants. The cookie contains a slip of paper with a message that reveals a secret about the future. Here's how to make fortune cookies containing personalised messages for your friends.

You Will Need:

• a piece of plain paper • scissors • pen or pencil • two baking trays • two egg whites • 35 g of plain flour • vanilla essence • a tablespoon and a teaspoon • a whisk • 50 g of granulated sugar • half a teaspoon of salt • yellow food colouring • greaseproof paper • a mixing bowl • a spatula • a mug • a wire rack • a sieve

WRITING YOUR SECRET MESSAGES

Think of the messages you want your cookies to contain – they could be predictions of your friends' futures, such as 'Next month you will find what you've been looking for.'

Alternatively, you could get each of your friends to reveal a secret, such as 'I have a crush on Robert' or 'I want to be the star of the Christmas play'. Write these messages on pieces of paper no bigger than 2 cm by 5 cm.

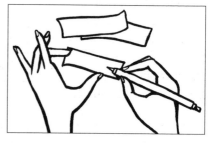

MAKING YOUR COOKIE BATTER

1. Preheat the oven to 150°C/ 300°F/ Gas Mark 2.

2. Whisk the egg whites and half a teaspoon of vanilla essence in a mixing bowl. When you are done, the mixture should be light and foamy.

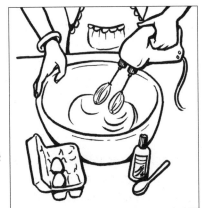

3. Sift the flour into the bowl with the sugar and the salt. Mix this into the egg whites and vanilla essence. Stir until smooth. To make your cookies extra special, add a few drops of yellow food colouring – the colour yellow signifies that being together with your friends makes you happy (for different colour codes, see pages 26–27).

4. Place two teaspoons of the batter about 10 cm apart on a sheet of greaseproof paper in a baking tray. Press each dollop with the back of a tablespoon to form flat, round cookie shapes, about 7 cm in diameter.

5. Put the cookies in the oven for five minutes, or until they are golden brown. Always ask an adult to help you when using an oven and always wear oven gloves.

6. While the first batch of cookies is in the oven, prepare a second batch using the other baking tray. You should always bake fortune cookies in batches like this, so that you have time to shape them before they cool down.

7. Take the first batch of cookies out of the oven. Use a spatula to remove each one from the tray and turn it upside down.

8. Place a paper 'fortune' in the centre of each cookie, and then fold the cookies in half.

9. Next, place the middle of a folded cookie across the rim of a mug. Gently push down each side of the cookie over the rim, as shown here, to make a little parcel. You'll need to work quickly so you can shape all of the cookies before they cool.

Warning. The cookies will still be hot when you are moulding them, so watch your fingers!

10. Remove your second batch of cookies from the oven, add the 'fortune' and shape them, too. Use up the rest of the batter by making more cookies in the same way.

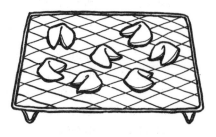

11. Lay your beautifully shaped cookies on a wire rack. When they are completely cool, hand them out to your friends to reveal their secrets, or predict their futures.

THE SECRET TO BEING A GOOD FRIEND

A true friend is hard to find – so make sure you keep your mates for life by being the best friend you can be. Here are some of the essential secrets of friendship.

• Share everything. Whether it's clothes, hopes and dreams, new friends or hobbies, or just crisps at break time, a good friend lives by the saying 'What's mine is yours'.

• Don't judge your friend for having different tastes from you. Having lots of things in common is fun, but liking different things is cool, too. Take advantage of your differences to learn about new things from each other. If you show an interest in your friend's hobbies, she might show an interest in yours.

• If your friend trusts you enough to tell you something

very personal about herself, you must listen carefully to what she is saying. Try to imagine exactly how she is feeling about what is happening to her. This will help you to be sympathetic and to offer sound advice.

• Take the time to tell your friend how much she means to you – she may not know just how special she is. If you know she is feeling down, give her lots of compliments and treat her like a princess for the day.

• Never forget a friend's birthday – make a special note of the date in your diary. Make her a card by printing out a photo of her and sticking it on some card. Why not add some magazine pictures of her favourite celebrities to form a collage and add some star quality. If you really want to impress her, bake her a birthday cake and decorate it with her favourite sweets – you'll be in her good books for weeks.

• Don't be a 'fair-weather friend' – someone who is only around to share the fun times, and disappears when the going gets tough. If you are a good friend, you will stick by your pal through thick and thin.

• Never lie to each other. It will break the trust that binds you together. If you are always honest, your friend will respect your opinion and forgive you, even if you say things she doesn't want to hear.

HOW TO HIDE YOUR DIARY

Follow these devious dos and don'ts to make sure your diary's secrets stay safe.

DO make a 'decoy' – a fake diary that puts people off the trail of the real thing. Write the word 'DIARY' in big letters on a brightly coloured book and scribble some convincingly 'false' entries inside it. This should fool any snoopers into thinking it's the real deal.

DO hide your diary inside another book when you want to write in it. If anyone asks what you are doing, you can pretend to be doing your homework.

DON'T remove your diary from its hiding place unless you want to write in it. Never carry it around in your bag. If someone discovers it, your secrets will be literally 'out of the bag' in no time.

DON'T hide your diary under your pillow – it's far too obvious. Instead, try tucking it inside the pocket of an old coat that you never wear. Hang it at the back of your wardrobe. No one will think to look there.

HOW TO PLAY THE SHADOWING GAME

Spies are trained in the art of tailing a target without being noticed. To see if you've got what it takes to become a spy, play the Shadowing Game with your friends and see if you can become as silent and unnoticeable as a shadow.

HOW TO PLAY

1. Arrange to go on a shopping trip with five of your friends. Ask everyone to wear a wristwatch and bring a notebook and pen.

2. Divide up into two groups of three. Two people will be the 'targets' (one will be 'target A' and the other 'target B'). The remaining person will be the 'spy'.

3. Synchronise watches – make sure your watches all say the same time – and agree to meet up again in exactly thirty minutes. During this time, the targets must walk around the shopping centre together, while the spy has to track their movements – without being noticed. The two targets are free to wander from shop to shop. They don't have to stick together all the time, but they must remain in the same shop as each other.

TRACKING POINTS

If the spy successfully follows both targets without being seen for a whole thirty minutes, she wins a point. An extra point is given if the spy has successfully logged the exact movements of both target A and target B in her notebook. Here's an example of the kinds of things a spy might write down:

SATURDAY

10 am. Targets leave the sweet shop and head for the bench. They sit down and eat sweets from a paper bag.
10.10 am. Targets get up and walk towards the perfume shop. Targets try two different perfumes.
10.16 am. Targets leave perfume shop and go to the charity shop. Targets go into changing rooms.
10.27 am. Targets come out of changing rooms. Target A buys a navy blue woolly jumper. Target B buys a small yellow handbag. Targets leave shop to return to meeting point.

Repeat the game until everybody has had a chance to be a spy. The spy with the most points wins the game.

TIPS FOR SUCCESSFUL SHADOWING

If you find that your targets are spotting you too often, it's time to learn some serious spy tactics.

- As soon as the game has begun, find somewhere in the shop to hide that is a 'safe' distance from your targets – behind a window display or curtain, for instance. If a target stops or turns around suddenly, you should be far enough away to remain unnoticed.

- Bring a long coat with you to the shops. Quickly slip it on to avoid your targets recognising you instantly if they do spot you. You'll find more quick ways to disguise your identity on pages 68–69.

- To prevent your footsteps echoing down a hallway and blowing your cover, tread as softly and quietly as you can. Wearing soft-soled trainers and walking on tiptoes will help you to avoid discovery.

- Carry a small compact mirror in your pocket. When your target is directly behind you, pretend to re-apply your lipstick using the mirror, angling it so that you can see the reflection of your targets in the glass. If they move out of the shop, you will see them go.

- Carry a prop, such as an umbrella or a newspaper, so you can use it to cover your face if they look your way.

- Wear dark sunglasses to avoid any possibility of eye contact. Even if the target catches your eye, look away and pretend to be interested in something else, such as the contents of a shop window display, or a dress on a clothes rail.

THE SECRET TO BEING POLITE

Polite girls know the secret to being a good guest. Leave a good impression wherever you go with these shining examples of politeness.

Write Thank You Letters. If someone has given you a gift, always thank them with a card or letter. Make it personal by explaining what you will use the gift for, or how it will be useful to you. For example: *Thank you for the paint set. I can't wait to use it to paint a picture while I am on holiday.*

Thank People For Their Hospitality. If you've been to a friend's for tea or overnight, don't skip out of the door without thinking. Always thank your friend's parents for letting you visit.

Don't Make Noise Pollution. If you're in a library or a cinema, always switch your mobile phone to silent and keep your music down on your MP3 player. If someone asks you to be less noisy when you're laughing with your mates, be respectful.

Remember Your Table Manners. Never talk with your mouth full, or reach rudely over someone else's plate to get the salt. Always remember to thank the chef for cooking a delicious meal.

HOW TO MAKE A SECRET BOOK SAFE

Do you need a top-secret hiding place for your diary? Here's an old classic you could try. It's time to get seriously sneaky ...

You Will Need:

• an old hardback book that is bigger and thicker than your diary (have a look in your local charity shop for the oldest-looking one you can find) • a sheet of card • scissors

1. Draw a rectangle on a piece of card, 2 cm smaller than the size of a page in the big hardback book. Cut it out to make your template.

2. Open the book near the beginning and fold three or four pages in half, as shown. Place your template on top of the folded pages and draw round it.

3. Now cut the folded pages along the outline you have drawn.

4. Repeat steps 2 and 3 until there are only a few intact pages left of your book. Place your diary inside the hole in your book and close the cover.

5. Finally, put your fake book on the bookshelf among all the others – no one will have any idea what is inside it.

THE SECRET TO KEEPING NEW YEAR'S RESOLUTIONS

Deciding to quit a bad habit or learn a new skill is a brilliant idea at the beginning of a brand new year. If, however, your good intentions are starting to slip, you need to know the secret to sticking to your New Year's resolutions.

Keep Your List Short. Don't write a list of ten resolutions. Decide on two or three you really want to achieve and stick to them.

Stuck For Resolutions? Pick two from this list of ready-made New Year's resolutions and stick to them like your life depended on it!

NEW YEAR'S RESOLUTIONS

- Spend more time with Mum
- Argue less with my brothers/sisters
- Eat 5 pieces of fruit a day
- Do my homework on time
- Watch less TV • Learn to Salsa dance
- Read more books • Ride my bike to school

Be Realistic. If you don't play guitar, don't vow that you will be a guitar player in a band by the end of the year. Break your resolution down into smaller chunks – for instance, 'Save up for my own guitar'.

Be Positive. Don't write down negative things that you shouldn't do – you will only want to rebel against them. For example, instead of saying 'I won't bite my nails ever again', say 'I will look after my nails and enjoy using lots of pretty nail varnish'.

Have A Thought For Others. Research suggests that you are far more likely to stick to your resolutions if they benefit or help other people. For example, promising to spend more time with your mum will not only be good for your relationship, your mum will enjoy it, too.

Get Support From Friends. Are you keen to save your pocket money? Instead of resolving not to buy sweets on your way home from school, why not make the last Friday of every month *Bake Day*? Pool your money together with a friend to buy cake mixture and make delicious cakes together.

Keep A Progress Calendar. For each week that you have kept to your resolution, stick a star or draw a smiley face on a calendar – this will spur you on.

HOW TO PASS ON A SECRET MESSAGE

You have something to tell a friend, but you can't risk anyone finding out what it is. Here are some ways you and your friend can keep information strictly confidential.

AN UNASSUMING ARTICLE

Writing Undercover. Start reading a newspaper article. Using a fine pen, make a dot the size of a pinprick under each letter of each word in your secret message. Make sure that you make a dot under each letter in the exact order that it appears in your message. Now pass the newspaper on to your friend and tell her that there is an interesting article on page [*insert page number here*]. By writing down each letter that has a dot underneath it, in the order that it appears, your secret message is revealed.

A Sticky Secret. Tell your friend you want to lend her a book that you know she would enjoy reading. Before you give it to her, write your secret message on a sticky note and pop it in the middle of one of the pages, about half way through the book. When she eventually gets to the page with the sticky note on, she will discover your secret message.

DEAD-LETTER DROP

In The Frame. Next time you need to tell your friend a secret, simply find a photo of the two of you and pop it in a frame. Be sure to position the photo so that it is slightly wonky in the frame. Hide your secret letter behind the photo and present the frame to your friend. Use the frame in future to hide secret messages – your friend will know there is a new message every time she spots that the photo is wonky.

A Ribbon Reaction. Pass on a secret message to your friend without even being in the same room as her! Simply tell your friend that a letter containing a secret message, for her eyes only is located in the park, near to a red ribbon.

When no one is looking, hide the letter behind the swings in the park. Tie a red ribbon to the swing's poles to alert your friend she has the right spot. When you have planted the letter, go home and text your friend to tell her your secret letter is ready for pick-up.

Warning. Always tell an adult where you are going and never go to the park on your own after dark.

HOW TO FORM A SECRET SOCIETY

Forming a secret society can lead to lots of brilliant adventures. Here's how to set up the most 'top-secret' of clubs, but be warned – everyone will want to be a member!

INVITE MEMBERS

Only invite your most trusted friends to join your society – the ones who have shown that they are good at keeping secrets.

You will need to send out invitations with details about when and where your first meeting will be held. To keep things top secret, write invisibly on each invitation (see pages 82–83 for ways to write invisibly).

Give away as little information as possible on each invitation. Invent a code name for yourself and your members to keep your identities private.

Your presence is requested for a top-secret meeting at my house at 4.30 pm. Please ensure you are not followed.

Bring along one idea for our club's name. Do not write it down.

You will be sent a password by text message at 6pm today. Please state this password upon arrival.

Miss Pink

CHOOSE A SECRET PASSWORD

You'll need the secret password for members to use to gain access to the society. Use an unusual word for the password, such as WOMBAT or FIZZ-POP. Give a time on your invitation for when you will send out this password. At exactly the time you stated, send a text message with only the password in it.

YOUR FIRST MEETING

On the day of your meeting, leave a notepad and pencil outside your front door. When each member arrives, ask them to write down the secret password on a piece of paper and post it through the letter box. If they have the correct password, let them in. If they don't know the password, don't open the door.

At your first ever meeting you will need to decide who should be the chairperson – this is the person who leads the meeting and makes sure that everyone gets a chance to speak. You should also choose the member with the neatest handwriting to write the 'minutes' – these are a record of the most important things that happen during the meeting.

NAME GAME

When you are all together, ask everyone to tell the group what they think the club should be called. Put it to a vote and the name that gets the highest number of votes wins. Why not suggest a couple of names to get the ideas flowing, such as *The Secret Sisterhood* or *Damsels Who Dare*?

LOGO LOGIC

If your club is going to be taken seriously, it needs to establish its own secret identity. Design a logo – this is a simple picture that sums up the spirit of your club. Draw the logo on any message that reveals club business, for example, when passing secret messages about the next club meeting.

CLUB RULES

Club rules are there to make sure your society stays a secret. Make each member read your club's rules and swear to obey them. Here are the most important rules for members to follow:

- Never talk about the society in front of, or within earshot of, non-members.

- Only refer to other members using their code names.

- Check that you are not being followed when going to a meeting.

- Safety comes first – never undertake secret missions that will put you or anyone else in any danger.

THE SECRET TO NATURAL BEAUTY

The secret to looking your best is to be 'comfortable in your own skin' – this means not striving to look like someone else. Allow your natural beauty to shine through. Read on to discover how to reveal the best in you ... your friends will soon be wondering what your secret is.

WORK WITH WHAT YOU'VE GOT

• If you are pale, don't burn yourself in the sun trying to tan – enjoy your pale and stunning beauty and apply sunscreen every day to protect your delicate skin. If you have dark skin, you are lucky and can wear bright, vibrant colours to show it off.

• If you are blessed with curly hair, forget straighteners and wear your ringlets loud and proud. If your hair is poker straight, experiment with funky clips or scrape your hair back into an extra high and bouncy ponytail.

• Avoid smothering your skin in too much make-up. Give your skin air to breath and show the world you are a true natural beauty – see page 16 for ways to wear less make-up and still look beautiful.

ENERGISE WITH EXERCISE

You will not only look better after doing exercise, but you will feel on top of the world, too. Put on your favourite album and dance like crazy for fifteen minutes. Do this once a day to really see the benefits – your skin should look brighter and

you will have more energy. Alternatively, get down to the park or out in the garden with a friend and make yourself a fitness circuit. Divide the grass into three different areas using twigs or stones. In each area, you can perform a different activity. For example, one area could be for doing star jumps, another could be for skipping and another for jogging on the spot. Take it in turns to spend five minutes in each area, performing the relevant activity. When the five minutes are up, move on to the next area.

BEAUTY SLEEP

Every girl needs her beauty sleep to make her look and feel her best. When you are fast asleep your body is secretly hard at work repairing skin cells, making your skin fresh and bright for when you wake up. Aim to have around eight hours' sleep a night – see page 102 for tips on how to get the perfect night's sleep. You will find you have more energy to sparkle from the inside.

HOW TO TELL IF SOMEONE HAS READ YOUR DIARY

Your diary isn't quite where you left it. Has someone been taking a peek? Here are some tricks you can use to catch those sneaky snoopers out.

Not A Hair Out Of Place. Take one of your hairs – you will find tons in your hairbrush. Tuck one end of it between the cover of your diary and the first page. Tuck the other end between the last page and the back cover. Pop your diary in its usual hiding place. Next time you look, the hair should still be in place. If it isn't, you know that somebody has been nosing around where they are not welcome.

A Powdery Plot. Sprinkle some talcum powder onto the last page you have written on in your diary. Only sprinkle a tiny amount, so that it is hardly noticeable. Close the diary and go about your business. If someone has been snooping, the next time you look, you'll notice that the powder has fallen onto the floor near your diary's hiding place.

Suggestions For Snoopers. Write a false entry in your diary. If, for example, you think it is your little brother who is reading your diary, write something like, 'I wish [Ben] would buy me some sweets from the shop every now and then I would definitely let him use my computer.' If your brother miraculously starts buying you sweets, you're on to him.

THE SECRET TO CHANGING YOUR PARENTS' MINDS

Are you after some extra pocket money? Do you desperately want to be allowed to go to your friend's sleepover on a school night? Whatever you want to convince your parents of, here's how to do it:

CLEVER TACTICS

Flattery Will Get You Everywhere. Even if your dad comes downstairs dressed in a Hawaiian shirt that had its best days in the seventies, tell him he looks really cool. Parents love to be complimented.

Be The Model Daughter For A Week. Do your homework as soon as you get home from school and, after dinner, get up first and clear everyone's plates away – then do the washing up. It won't be the most fun week of your life, but if it gets your parents to change their minds, it'll be worth it.

Write A Report. Detail the points 'for' and 'against' being allowed to do something, in a formal-looking written report. Call a family meeting to discuss your report. Without getting upset or angry, clearly argue your case.

DESPERATE MEASURES

If the tactics above still haven't changed your parents' minds, then it's time to show them you mean business.

Make A Placard. Attach a piece of card to a stick with some tape. Write your demands on the card, such as 'I WANT MORE POCKET MONEY. WHEN DO I WANT IT ... NOW!' March up and down the living room waving your placard and singing this chant until your parents agree ... if only to shut you up!

A Vow Of Silence. Tell your parents that you have decided not to speak until they agree to your demands. Don't even crack when your brother uses your computer without asking.

The Sympathy Vote. Widen your eyes and bite your lower lip. Hang your head down and make as if you are going to cry. If you can, squeeze a few tears out – this takes practice.

Go On Strike. If all else fails – go on strike. Tie yourself to the sofa in protest, claiming that until your parents agree to your demands, you shall not be moved.

Warning. It is important to bear in mind these methods may actually make your parents less likely to change their minds.

HOW TO MAKE A CODED FRIENDSHIP BRACELET

Make a friendship bracelet for your best friend that conceals a unique colour-coded message. Use the colour chart on pages 26–27 to select three colours that sum up your friendship. Make a bracelet in these colours and let your mate know just how special she is to you.

MAKING FRIENDSHIP BRACELETS

You Will Need:

• card (roughly 25 cm by 25 cm) • soft embroidery thread in three different colours • scissors

1. Cut six pieces of thread, each one roughly a metre in length. You need two lengths of each colour. Knot them all together at one end. Leave 10 cm of loose thread hanging down after the knot.

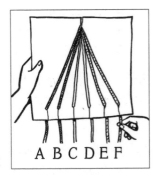

2. Make one 5-cm-long slit at the top of the piece of card. At the bottom cut six 5-cm-long slits, each roughly two centimetres apart.

3. Place the knotted end of your threads through the top slit. Separate the threads out and pull one through each of the bottom slits, keeping the colours in pairs, as shown.

4. Pull thread A over thread B.

51

5. Pull A back under B to make a knot, as shown. Slide the knot to the top of the threads. Move B back to the left-hand side. Repeat so that thread A forms another knot.

6. Now, move each thread along one slit to the left as this will help to keep your threads separated.

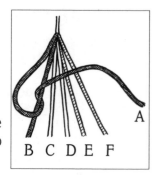

7. Continue to make two knots with thread A over each of the remaining threads, until A is on the far right-hand side, as shown.

8. Now repeat steps 4 to 7 with thread B.

9. Repeat, steps 4 to 7 with thread C, then D, then E, then F. Then start again with thread A. You will see that you are making pretty stripes with the threads.

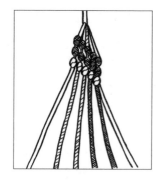

10. When your bracelet is long enough to go around your wrist, knot all the threads together, leaving about 10 cm of thread after the knot.

MAKING CODE BEADS

Add a personal message to the bracelet by making 'code beads'.

You Will Need:

- a baking tray • a large mixing bowl and 3 smaller bowls
- 50 g of salt • 150 g of plain flour, sieved • 150 ml of
lukewarm water • 3 plastic food bags • 3 skewers • PVA glue
and a small brush • petroleum jelly • food colouring in three
different colours • paper and pen • sequins • glitter

1. Draw a colour chart on a piece of paper, giving a specific
meaning to each shade of food colouring you have. For example:

Purple = Thank you for helping me with my homework.
Orange = You bake the yummiest cakes.
Turquoise = You are always incredibly kind to others.

2. Stir together the salt and flour.
Slowly add the water, constantly
stirring until you have mixed a soft
dough. Knead it with your hands
until smooth.

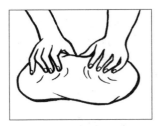

3. Divide the dough into three small bowls and add a few drops
of food colouring to each bowl. Mix the colour in to the dough.

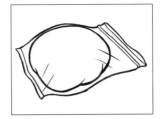

4. Place the three colours of dough
into separate plastic bags. Leave
them to sit for 30 minutes in a warm
room – this will help the dough to
bind together, making it easier to
shape later on.

5. Next, tear off a small piece of one colour of dough. Roll it with your palms to make a small dough ball. Repeat with each colour of dough to make three different-coloured beads. (Use up any excess dough to make extra beads – you could use them later to make a bracelet for yourself!)

6. Grease each skewer with petroleum jelly – this prevents the beads from sticking to the skewers. Push each bead onto a different skewer. Press a selection of sequins into each bead.

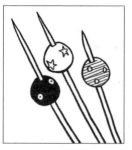

7. Balance the skewers across a baking tray. Bake the beads in the oven for between 30 minutes at 150ºC/ 300ºF/ Gas Mark 2, or until they are hard.

Warning. Ask an adult to help you when using the oven and always wear oven gloves.

8. When they are cool enough to touch, slide the beads off the skewers. Brush a thin layer of PVA glue over the beads to make them shiny. Mix the glue with some glitter to give your beads some extra sparkle.

9. When the glue has dried, thread your code beads onto the remaining threads hanging down on the bracelet. Secure them with a large knot. Leave 10 cm of loose thread hanging down after the knot – your friend will need this to tie the bracelet to her wrist.

10. Finally, wrap up your bracelet in the paper colour chart you prepared earlier, and present the gift to your friend.

HOW TO TELL SOMEONE A SECRET

It's not always a good idea to bottle up your emotions. Sometimes, telling somebody how you feel about something can help a situation rather than make it worse. If you feel that confiding in somebody is the best thing to do, then follow these four golden rules of telling a secret.

RULE ONE. Never tell someone a secret via email or by texting them. You could accidentally send the message to the wrong person, or your friend could forward your message to someone else by mistake. It is always better to tell secrets face-to-face.

RULE TWO. Make sure that you are confiding in the right person. Do you trust her to take your secret seriously, or is she the sort of person who makes a joke out of everything? Secrets are sometimes best told to an adult whom you know cares about you and your life.

RULE THREE. Pick your time carefully. A good time to tell a secret is when you are on your own with that person and you know that you are not going to be interrupted. It could be when you are walking home from school together, or a moment with your mum when everyone else is out.

RULE FOUR. Make sure that the person you are talking to understands that you are entrusting her with something private. It is for that person's ears only. If she knows that this is important to you, she will be less likely to blab.

HOW TO PLAY THE SECRET MISSION GAME

The Secret Mission Game is great to play at someone's birthday party, as the prize can be something really fun. Set up a trail of clues that need to be solved, which lead your friends to a secret location of your choice – where you will have laid on a prize. The game takes some preparation. Here's how to play.

CLUE-SOLVING MISSION

1. Before the game begins, decide on a secret location at which you want your friends to end up. This could be in the park, or the garden, or anywhere big enough for you to play games. Hide a box of games under a tree in your secret location. Fill it with skipping ropes, badminton rackets and things to pamper your friends with.

2. Write out the clues and hide them in advance. Each one should lead to the next. For example, the first clues could include:

CLUE ONE. The next clue is found near a watery place full of precious marine life. [Hide the next clue near the goldfish bowl.]

CLUE TWO. Look for the stars of the film *Watership Down*. [Hide the next clue in the rabbit hutch.]

CLUE THREE. Find the tallest tree in the garden. [Hide the next clue in the boughs of the tallest tree.]

CLUE FOUR. The next clue is nice and cold. [Hide it at the back of the fridge.]

CLUE FIVE. Careful not to sit on the next clue! [Hide the next clue under the sofa cushions.]

In the last clue that you hide, reveal the exact location where you want everybody to end up.

3. Next, gather your friends together in your bedroom. Hand each person a sealed envelope with 'Top Secret' written on the front. Inside should be identical messages detailing the mission and the first clue:

Dear Miss Pink,

Your secret mission is to find and solve a series of clues. If you solve all the clues correctly, you will successfully discover the secret location where games will begin! You have exactly forty-five minutes to complete your mission, after which time the fun will commence.

Your first clue is in this envelope. Good luck!

Get to your secret location early and set up your party games. Give everybody a party popper to congratulate them on successfully completing the mission.

THE SECRET TO UNDERSTANDING YOUR MUM

Even though you love your mum, it's easy to misunderstand each other. Below are the top five secrets every girl should know about their mum.

SECRET ONE. Mums love a chat. You don't have to tell her every single thing that you do, but try to include her in your life more. Tell her what's going on at school and how you are getting on with your friends.

SECRET TWO. Mums can have off days, just like you and your friends. If you think your mum is having a bad day, why not give her a big hug to show her how much you love her and that you care about her feelings?

SECRET THREE. Help Her Out. Don't argue if your mum asks you to do something. Instead, think about why she wants you to do it. For example, if she keeps asking you not to leave your towel on the bathroom floor, remember to pick it up and hang it on the hook – this way it won't have to be washed so often.

SECRET FOUR. Spend Some Quality Time. Cook a meal, sort through old photographs or do some gardening together. The more time you spend hanging out together, the more comfortable you will feel in each other's company.

SECRET FIVE. Listen To Her Advice. Your mum will have learnt lots of life lessons that can be very useful to you. If you're worried about something, tell your mum – she may know exactly what you should do.

HOW TO MAKE A FALSE-BOTTOMED BOX

You Will Need:

- a cardboard box – it needs to be bigger than your diary
- a piece of card that is bigger than the bottom of your box • scissors • pencil

1. Place your diary inside the cardboard box.

2. Put the box on top of the piece of card and draw around the bottom with a pencil. Place your box to one side.

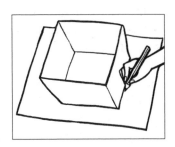

3. Draw another square within your box outline, roughly ½ cm smaller on each side. Cut out the inside square and throw away the rest of the card.

4. Fit this piece of card over your diary in the bottom of the box.

5. Finally, fill the box with old toys or clothes. Even if someone does go rifling through it to find your diary, they'll never succeed!

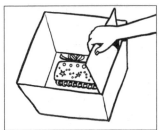

HOW TO DECODE PARENT SPEAK

Does it ever feel like your parents are talking in their own secret code? If you want to know what they really think, read on and find out the real meaning behind their words.

Your Parents Say: 'You're not going to watch that TV programme again. You know it's a load of rubbish.'
They Mean: 'I'm so glad you watch this – I secretly love it, too!'

Your Parents Say: 'It's important for you to learn how to do your own washing.'
They Mean: 'I have so much to do, it makes a real difference if you help me out.'

Your Parents Say: 'I'll think about it.'
They Mean: 'No.'

Your Parents Say: 'Would you mind making me a cup of tea?'
They Mean: 'I have had such a busy week, I need looking after for a change!'

Your Parents Say: 'I'm not helping you with your maths homework because it's important for you to work the answers out for yourself.'
They Mean: 'I'm not helping you because I can't even do simple addition without a calculator.'

Your Parents Say: 'We thought it would be nice for you to spend some quality time with your grandparents next weekend.'
They Mean: 'We need a break from you kids!'

THE SECRET TO BEATING THE BLUES

Are you feeling down in the dumps? Have you lost your sparkle? Don't fear – smart girls know there are ways to pick yourself up when you're feeling yucky. Here are their secrets:

DO treat yourself to a little chocolate. It boosts levels of a chemical called 'serotonin' that is naturally produced by your body. Serotonin helps to make you feel happy.

DON'T eat junk food as more than an occasional treat – it can make you feel sluggish.

DO take up a new hobby. Maybe join a drama group, or gym club – you might even make some new friends, too.

DON'T be a couch potato. Sitting around will make you feel worse. Get out to the park with your friends and feel instantly more refreshed and ready to face the world.

DO think positively. With a friend, write down five things you like about each other – it will give you a boost to see how much your friend values you.

HOW TO SPEAK A SECRET LANGUAGE

What could be more fun than bamboozling your parents and teachers by communicating with your friends in a secret language? Here are some tried and tested languages you could learn with your mates.

PIG LATIN

Pig Latin isn't really a type of Latin – it's just English with the letters swapped around. This is quite a tricky code to master, but it's extremely effective when spoken fast. Here's how:

- If a word begins with a vowel – that's a, e, i, o or u – then you add 'ay' on the end. For example, elephant becomes elephantay. Idiot becomes idiotay. Afternoon becomes afternoonay.

- If a word begins with a consonant – any letters that aren't vowels – then take the first letter of the word, move it to the end, and then add 'ay'. So, cat becomes atcay. Dog becomes ogday.

- If a word begins with two consonants, take them both and add them to the end of the word. Then add 'ay'. So, brilliant becomes illiantbray. Train becomes aintray. Phone becomes onephay.

Ancay ouyay eesay owhay tiay orksway?

Practise until you can form whole sentences without even thinking. You'll soon be able to chat in complete secrecy.

SECRET SLANG

Make up your own slang that only you and your friends can understand. Here are some words you can share.

Slang In Use Today	Made-Up Slang
This is **lush** = This is delicious.	Can I borrow your **pencil?** = The boy you fancy has just walked in the room!
I'm so **igry** = I'm so embarrassed.	Nice **nail varnish** = Teacher/parent alert.
You're **the bomb** = You're excellent!	**It's all sequins and buttons** = This is a secret.
I'm **flat roofin'** for my exams at the moment = I'm working hard for my exams.	It's such a **pink hairband day** today = I need looking after and pampering today.

THE PHONETIC ALPHABET

This phonetic alphabet was invented to help soldiers at war, allowing them to convey important messages accurately. In this alphabet, each letter is represented by a word. So if you need to tell someone a secret, spell it out with these words:

Alpha, Bravo, Charlie, Delta, Echo, Foxtrot,
Golf, Hotel, India, Juliet, Kilo, Lima, Mike,
November, Oscar, Papa, Quebec, Romeo, Sierra,
Tango, Uniform, Victor, Whiskey, X-ray, Yankee, Zulu

For example: Whiskey India Lima Lima India Alpha Mike
is looking so gorgeous today.

THE SECRET TO COPING WITH NERVES

Lots of different things make people nervous – flying on planes, the first day at a new school, visiting the dentist, giving a speech or sitting an exam. Here are some exercises you can practise that will banish the jitters and leave you feeling super-confident.

BREATHE IT OUT

People often breathe too fast when they are anxious, which has the effect of pumping extra oxygen around the body, making you jittery and light-headed. Breathing deeply instantly makes you feel calm and in control.

So next time you feel butterflies in your tummy, breathe slowly in through your nose, then slowly out again through the nose. Silently count 'one'. Then repeat the calm in-and-out breath through your nose, and count 'two'. Repeat up to ten. If you lose count, start again from one.

USE YOUR IMAGINATION

The day before the event you are nervous about, take some time to imagine yourself in the situation. If you are worried about sitting an exam, imagine yourself walking into the exam room feeling confident.

Imagine yourself feeling calm as you find your seat. Imagine feeling happy when you turn over the exam paper and the first question you see is one that you know the answer to! Before exam day, run through this scenario in your mind several times, each time picturing yourself feeling calm and confident. You'll feel ten times better when the time actually comes.

RELAX YOUR BODY

When you are nervous, often all your muscles will become tense, which makes you feel worse. To stop this from happening, silently run through each body part in your head – from your toes upwards – clench them tight then relax them. As you are doing this, slowly and calmly say to yourself, 'I relax my toes. My toes are relaxed.' Then move on to the next part. 'I relax my ankles. My ankles are relaxed.' And so on.

Be careful not to become so relaxed you nod off completely.

HOW TO DECODE THE SECRETS OF BODY LANGUAGE

Did you know that by examining the way someone uses their body, or their body language, it is sometimes possible to reveal the secrets of what they are thinking? Body language is a way we communicate without speaking. Some common gestures are decoded below.

MIRROR IMAGE

If someone mirrors your movements – that is, they seem to be copying you – it can mean that they like you, and want to show they are similar to you.
It can also mean they feel slightly nervous being around you.
Try to make them feel comfortable and at ease (for tips on how to do this, see page 113).

CROSSED ARMS

If someone has their arms crossed while you are talking to them, it could indicate that they are upset or angry with you. Beware what you say to them, as they might pick an argument with you at any moment.

HEAD TILT

Someone tilting their head is a subconscious way of showing you they are not dangerous or threatening. It can be seen in the way a mother talks to a young child. The tilt can also mean that what is being said is not meant to be taken seriously – they are joking with you.

OPEN PALMS

If someone holds the palms of their hands facing you while they are talking to you, it usually means that they are being open and honest. If they keep their palms apart, but their fingertips touching, this means they are trying to make you feel confident about what they are saying.

EYE CONTACT

Making eye contact – looking into someone's eyes – indicates that you feel comfortable around them. If someone tries to avoid making eye contact with you, you should suspect they may be telling you fibs. (See page 111 for more ways to detect if someone is not telling you the truth.)

HOW TO MAKE A SECRET DISGUISE

If you're playing the Shadowing Game (see pages 34–36) with friends who know you very well, you'll need to create a perfect disguise that allows you to trail them incognito. Here are some dos and don'ts of creating a disguise.

DON'T buy a disguise of the 'comedy moustache and glasses' type from a joke shop. Wearing this will make you stand out from the crowd more than ever.

DO style long hair, if you have it, into two plaits and curl these up into a hat to hide it. If you have short hair, why not wear a realistic-looking wig from a fancy-dress shop?

DON'T wear any items that people associate with you – such as your favourite hooded cardigan or new ballet pumps. Even pulling on your signature stripy socks will be a dead giveaway.

DO carry a prop that will draw attention away from your face. An umbrella on a wet day or a big sun hat when it's scorching hot are excellent, as you can hide underneath them.

DON'T walk in the same way that you usually walk, as people can often be recognised by their movements. Don't adopt a limp, however, as this will look suspicious and get you noticed. Instead, walk faster if you usually dawdle, and vice versa.

DO wrap a scarf around your neck and pull it up to cover the lower part of your face. Choose a scarf suitable to the season: woollen scarves look odd on a hot day. During warmer months, wrap a cotton scarf over your whole head, leaving a gap in the material around your eyes so that you can still see.

DON'T arouse suspicion by looking awkward in your disguise. Pulling off a disguise requires panache and confidence.

DO use make-up to transform your face. Use a light-brown coloured eyeliner pencil to dot 'freckles' over your nose and cheeks, or a dark brown pencil to make yourself a fake mole.

HOW TO PLAY THE SECRET SLEEPOVER SURPRISE GAME

The Secret Sleepover Surprise Game is a version of a game that is often played at Christmas called 'Secret Santa'. In Secret Santa everybody is given a present but without the buyer, revealing her identity. In Secret Sleepover Surprise everyone is given a surprise gift and a pampering treat.

BEFORE YOUR GUESTS ARRIVE

Ask everyone coming to the sleepover to bring along a surprise gift – something they no longer want that is cool and in good condition. It could, for example, be a game or an item of clothing.

Cut out some little slips of paper – two for every person who will be coming to the party. Write each guest's name on a slip of paper. Fold them up very small so the names cannot be seen. Place the slips into a bowl or an upturned hat.

On the remaining slips of paper, write down some treats that will be promised to each guest – one treat on each slip of paper. Fold these up as before, and place them in a separate hat or bowl. Here are some ideas for treats:

- French plaiting hair • back massage • manicure or pedicure (including painting the nails) • makeover • fortune-telling • head massage • face mask

In a box, place all the items you need to perform the pampering tasks – for example, nail varnish (a variety of colours), make-up and brushes, hairbrush and hairbands, face mask or face pack, etc.

LET THE GAMES BEGIN

When your sleepover is under way, announce that you have a new game to play, and produce your two 'lucky dip' bowls. Each person in the room must then take a slip of paper from each pot. (If anyone happens to draw their own name, they must pick again and put that slip back into the bowl.)

Now each guest reads out the name and the treat on their slips of paper. The named person must hand that guest their surprise gift and perform the treat. This way everyone is guaranteed a great gift and some luxurious pampering.

THE SECRET TO BEING A GOOD LOSER

If you've ever been well and truly beaten at your favourite game, you'll know how hard it is to be on the losing side. Resist the temptation to stamp your feet and cry in frustration, your friends will rapidly lose respect for you. Instead, learn the secrets to losing in style.

AN ART COMPETITION

Have you found yourself coming last in an art competition? Don't criticise the winning painting – this will make you look bitter. Find three things you like about the winning entry and tell the people around you. Listen to the judge's criticisms of your work, taking them on board for next time. Promising yourself you'll enter again next year will spur you on to improve your technique. Learning from failure will help you succeed in the future.

A BIG GAME

If you lose a sporting event or a big game – for example, a netball match with another school – show that you respect the winners by shaking hands with every member of the winning team – even if you don't feel like it. This shows you admire their skills and recognise their achievement.

BE A WINNER

Be self-critical and take a look at the things you did wrong. If it was a dance competition, did you spend enough time practising? Did you stay up too late the night before, making you tired on the big day?

Losing can be good for you. People who end up winning the biggest prizes haven't won every competition they've ever entered. They have suffered knock backs and failures and bounced back stronger in order to reach the top.

Winning isn't everything – taking part is just as important. Whatever the outcome you still had fun, and there's always next time ...

HOW TO COMMUNICATE IN THE DARK

Morse code is a code used to communicate messages over long distances. It's an effective way to send secret messages in the dark, or over the phone. If your friend lives close enough to see her bedroom window, why not use Morse code to chat to each other?

HOW IT WORKS

Using just a torch, you can spell out the letters of a secret message using the Morse code alphabet below. Each letter of the alphabet is represented by a unique pattern of dots and/or dashes. When using torches, a short flash represents a dot and a dash is represented by a longer flash. If you don't have a torch, you could switch your bedroom light on and off.

A . _	J . _ _ _	S . . .	2 . . _ _ _
B _ . . .	K _ . _	T _	3 . . . _ _
C _ . _ .	L . _ . .	U . . _	4 . . . . _
D _ . .	M _ _	V . . . _	5 . . . . .
E .	N _ .	W . _ _	6 _ . . . .
F . . _ .	O _ _ _	X _ . . _	7 _ _ . . .
G _ _ .	P . _ _ .	Y _ . _ _	8 _ _ _ . .
H	Q _ _ . _	Z _ _ . .	9 _ _ _ _ .
I . .	R . _ .	1 . _ _ _ _	0 _ _ _ _ _

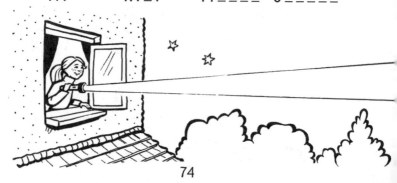

Each new word in a message is indicated by turning the light off completely for the length of time it takes to say the word 'dit' five times.

Top Tip. To keep the length of your flashes consistent, say the word 'dit' during a short flash (turn off the light when you finish saying 'dit') and for long dashes, say 'daah' in your head.

SENDING A MESSAGE IN MORSE CODE

Write out the Morse code opposite on a piece of paper for your friend. At exactly 9.50 pm send your friend a blank text message to make sure she is ready to receive your message (see page 78 for more ways to text in code). If she replies 'Yes', send the message below from your bedroom window (brackets are used to show individual words).

(..) (_./././_..) (_/ _ _ _) (_/./_./_..) (_._ _/_ _ _/._) (._)
(.../././_._./._/_/_./_/)

Translation: I need to tell you a secret.

You can also practise transmitting a Morse code message using a whistle in the playground. Simply blow a short blast for a dot and a longer blast for a dash.

75

THE SECRET TO SAYING YOU'RE SORRY

Saying sorry isn't easy – it's hard to admit you have been in the wrong. If you want to say sorry and show that you really mean it, taking the trouble to find an original way of doing it will show someone you're sincere. Here are some things you could do.

Make A Poster. Write an apologetic message in big, bold letters on an A3 piece of card, such as: 'Dear Dad, I'm sorry! Love from [*your name*]'. Hang the poster somewhere your dad will find it as an unexpected surprise, such as on the garden gate where he will see it on the way to work, or beside the bathroom mirror that he uses when he shaves in the mornings.

The Biggest Sorry Ever. Spell out the word 'SORRY' in big letters using unusual materials. You could use stones or twigs to make the word on a lawn, or shells and seaweed on the beach. Alternatively, use kitchen items such as cutlery or milk bottle tops arranged on the dining table to spell out your apology.

Top Tip. If the person you want to say sorry to is not around, take a photo of your handiwork on your mobile and text it to them.

Write A Poem. Make someone laugh by giving them a card with a rhyming apology inside. Decorate the front of the card using glitter pens, if you have them. Inside, write a poem in which the first letter of every line spells out the word sorry.

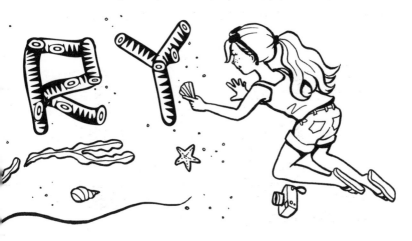

Saturday was a horrid day
Only because we rowed
Realising I hurt your feelings made me
Really sad all day
You and I should be best friends all the way!

Alternatively, make someone laugh with a silly rhyme.

This is a message for you, dear friend
I hope we can make a happy end
I'm really sorry that I was bad
Now please stop being so mad.

THE SECRET LANGUAGE OF

❸ ⓪ ⑤ ☊ ⓪ ⑤ ～ ⑩ :-)

It's easy to send secret messages via text or email. Arrange with your friends to send texts or emails using just these codes to keep your messages completely private.

TRICKY TEXT TALK

Here are some text techniques:

• Write sentences backwards to confuse anyone snooping through your inbox: 'This like, backwards write you where messages text coded use to friends your with arrange'.

• Disguise the meanings of your messages by writing out a key, like the one below, and circulate it among your friends:

1. A blank text message means, 'I have a secret to tell you. Come round to my house when you're free.'

2. A text message containing only the letter 'X' means there is an emergency secret meeting after school.

3. A text message containing two exclamation marks means, 'I feel sad today and need cheering up.'

4. A text message with the letter 'O' repeated six times means I have bought you a present.

5. A blank text message sent at exactly 9.50 pm means, 'Are you awake? I am about to send a Morse code message so look out of your bedroom window' (see pages 74-75 for how to communicate in Morse code).

WINGDING WEIRDNESS

If you want to send a message via email, or keep a secret diary on your computer, disguise the words with an unusual font. Here's how:

Simply type the message into an email. Now highlight all the words. Then select 'wingdings' as the font in which the words should appear (any other symbol font will also work). Your message will transform into odd-looking symbols like this:

'Do you want to take my dog for a walk with me this afternoon?' becomes:

➥⑥ ❺⑥❶ ❸⌦⑤❺⓿ ⓿⑥ ⓿⌦②↝ ④❺ ⌦⑥↝ ↝⑥⑨ ⌦
❸⌦❸② ❸⓪⓿↝ ④↝ ⓿↝⓿⑩ ⌦↝⓿↝⑨⑤⑥⑥⑤↝

To read your message, your friend must highlight the text and change it back to a readable font, such as 'Times New Roman' or 'Gill Sans'.

EMOTICONS

Most mobiles have an option to insert a smiley face (known as an emoticon) to add extra emotion to your messages. Make up your own secret emoticons to share with friends. Here are some to use – look at them sideways to get the picture:

/5 = High five on your exam results
(::():::) = I'll always be there for you
:-§ = Keep this a secret
8-] = I have a crush on that person
:-@ = My little brother makes me scream
({) = I want to give you a big hug
: ' -) = That joke made me cry with laughter.

THE SECRET TO UNDERSTANDING TEACHERS

Are you desperate to get in your teachers' good books but whatever you do you just can't seem to make them happy? Here's a guide to what's really going on in their heads.

SECRET SUBTEXT

Your Teachers Say: 'I've got a fun little project for you all to be getting on with today!'
They Mean: 'You're going to be spending this morning tidying up the stock cupboard.'

Your Teachers Say: 'I thought this afternoon we could do silent reading.'
They Mean: 'I've got a headache and need you all to be quiet today.'

Your Teachers Say: 'I'm only going to say this once.'
They Mean: 'I don't want to end up repeating this four times because half of you aren't listening.'

Your Teachers Say: 'Let's look up the answer to your question on the computer together.'
They Mean: 'I haven't got the foggiest what the answer is!'

Your Teachers Say: 'Today we'll be watching a DVD.'
They Mean: 'I left my lesson plan at home today.'

Your Teachers Say: 'I would never have behaved like that when I was at school.'
They Mean: 'I can't quite remember my school days now.'

TEACHER'S PET

If you already have a good relationship with your teacher but don't wish to be labelled as a teacher's pet, stick to the advice below:

- Vary where you sit in the classroom each day. You don't have to sit right next to the teacher to answer questions and be actively involved in the lesson.

- Let your classmates answer some questions – even though you know the answers to all of them.
Your teacher will see that you know them, too, when she marks your homework.

- Put your hand up and ask your teacher to explain something again if you don't understand. Your friends will be impressed by your honesty and grateful for the opportunity to have it explained again.

HOW TO WRITE INVISIBLY

Have a go at writing invisible messages that only your friends
will know how to reveal. Use a different method of writing
invisibly each time, to put off any snoopers who think they've
cracked how to reveal your messages.

WET WRITING

1. Soak a sheet of plain paper
in water. Lay it on a table.

2. Carefully place a dry sheet
of paper directly on top of it.

3. Using a ballpoint pen, write
your message on the dry sheet.

4. Peel off the dry top sheet
and throw it in the bin. Let the
wet sheet underneath dry.

5. When the wet sheet has
dried, give it to your friend.
Instruct her that all she has to
do to reveal the secret message
is wet the paper again,
and voilà!

Top Tip. Always send a text message to your friend before you
give her an invisible message to tell her the method you are
using to write invisibly. For wet writing, text the word 'Wet'.

CHEMICAL REACTION

1. Mix equal amounts of water and baking soda together in a bowl.

2. Dip a toothpick into the mixture and, using it as a pen, write your secret message on a piece of white paper.

3. Send your friend the text message 'Grape'. This will tell her to reveal your message she must brush some grape juice over the paper (you can buy cartons of grape juice in the supermarket). The chemicals in the baking soda and grape juice react together to change the colour of your message to brown.

COCOA CODING

1. On a piece of white paper, write your message using the end of a white wax candle as your pencil.

2. Send your friend the text message 'Wax'. To reveal the writing, she should sprinkle a fine layer of cocoa powder over the paper and dust it off. The message will magically appear.

THE SECRET TO BEING A WINNER

Most of life's winners have a positive mental attitude that gets them to the top. When others are wondering what to watch on TV in the evening, winners are focused on their future successes. Read on to fathom the formula for success.

POSITIVE THINKING

The power of positive thinking means that you have to believe that you can win. Get it right and you'll spend more time seeing the prizes mount up on top of your set than watching what's on TV.

If you're determined to win the three-legged race on sports day, for example, focus on the reasons why you want to win. Write them down. This year might mean that you'll have won that race five years in a row, or you may have never won anything in your life before. You may want to win something with your best friend to remember forever.

The night before the race, lie back and concentrate really hard. Picture your reasons for wanting to win the race in your head, focusing on each one-by-one. Picture yourself crossing the finish line way ahead of the opposition and see yourself being handed a trophy. On the day of the race you will be so motivated, you might just have what it takes to come in first.

BE IN IT TO WIN IT

Winners never shy away from a competition. They enter everything in the belief that winning is within their grasp.

So next time your friend asks you to enter the science competition at school, say yes, even if you know that the year above is competing, too. You never know, the judges may be bored by seeing the same old thing every year and be so impressed by your entry that they put you in first place.

DON'T GO WITH THE FLOW

Instead of doing things the same way everyone has done them before, winners often look out for opportunities to challenge themselves and do things differently.

So it's time for you to stop going with the flow. For example, have your friends ever complained that there is nowhere to play together after school? Why not draw up a plan for a youth club in your home town. Submit it to your local council. The council might be so impressed by your initiative that you and your friends win yourselves a brand new youth club. Think big ideas. Think original ideas. Think like a winner.

THE SECRETS REVEALED BY YOUR HANDWRITING

To find out what your friends are really like, sneak a peek at their homework. The style of handwriting can speak volumes about their personalities.

Large Letters
This indicates the writer is outgoing and confident – at least she appears to be, it could just be an act.

abcdef

abcdef

Upright Letters
This person is happy to be alone and can cope with pressure well.

Letters Slanted To The Left
This person can be guilty of keeping themselves to themselves and blocking others out.

abcdef

Small Letters
The writer likes pondering on life, and is good at school work. She may be quite shy or quiet.

abcdef

Messy Writing
This person may find it difficult to concentrate and may often be wrapped up in her own thoughts.

abcdef.

Neat Writing
This girl maybe quite considerate and reliable, but all may not be as it seems ... she could be a wild child at heart!

abcdef

Letters Slanted To The Right
This person likes to communicate with others and loves to party.

abcdef

THE SECRET TO SUCCESSFUL PUBLIC SPEAKING

Speaking in front of people – whether it's in the classroom, for a competition, or giving a speech in front of the whole school – is enough to give anyone the jitters. Successful public speakers know there are certain tricks to wowing their audiences and keeping their attention.

SPEECH-GIVING SECRETS

Here are some speech-giving secrets that every public speaker should have up her sleeve:

Eye Contact. Staring at some random spot in the distance while reading out your speech will only make your audience wonder if you are even bothered that they are there. Make eye contact with different people around the room throughout your speech to show you are interacting with them.

Project Your Voice. When speaking to a lot of people, in either a big room or hall, you need to 'project' your voice to make yourself heard. This does not mean you have to start shouting – it means that you should make your normal voice louder. Practise by trying it out at home first.

Transfix Your Audience. Make sure you know your speech off by heart. For maximum effect, deliver your speech in a slow and controlled manner – your audience will be transfixed by your every word.

Vary Your Voice. Don't speak in the same tone the whole way through. Make your voice quieter or louder to emphasise different points of the speech. This helps to draw attention to certain parts of what you are saying.

Prepare Prompt Cards. Don't write out everything you want to say and then read it out from a piece of paper with your head bent down the whole time. Prepare some 'prompt' cards. Cut out pieces of card that are roughly the same size as your palm. On these, write down the main points of your speech, adding key words and sentences to remind you what you were going to say about the points. When you are speaking, look up and at your audience – only glance down at the cards to jog your memory when necessary.

Make Them Laugh. A joke will make your audience sit up and take notice of what you have to say. Try to think of two good jokes, one to start and one to end your speech.

HOW TO MAKE A SECRET DEN

Dens are excellent places to hold secret meetings with your friends. Find out how to make your very own private den.

LOCATION, LOCATION, LOCATION

Dens come in all different shapes and sizes. You could easily convert any of the following places into a den that is big enough for you and your friends: a cupboard under the stairs, a large, rarely used wardrobe, a basement, the space under a tree with low-hanging branches or behind bushes in your back garden.

Simple dens only need some walls. If you're outside, stretch an old sheet over the top of two bushes and cover with twigs to camouflage it. If your den is indoors, stretch a sheet from the back of a sofa and anchor the other end with cushions.

THE RULES OF DEN-MAKING

RULE ONE. Secrecy is key. A successful den cannot be easily seen by passers-by, or stumbled upon by siblings.

RULE TWO. Never make a den anywhere that might be dangerous – remote woodland hideaways are not a good idea.

RULE THREE. Keep the entrance to your den small – this is a sure-fire way of keeping adults out.

RULE FOUR. Only tell your closest friends where it is located – this way you will keep it secret for longer.

DECORATE YOUR DEN

Here's how to make your den a twinkling Aladdin's cave:

You Will Need:

• a ball of string • a selection of buttons, beads, old CDs,
sweet wrappers and milk bottle tops • dressmaker's scissors
• fabric in bright colours

1. Cut six pieces of string, each one a metre long. Tie a big
knot at the end of each piece of string and secure with a big
bead. Cut a longer piece of string, roughly 5 m long.

2. Make small holes in the milk bottle tops and thread them
on to each of the shorter pieces of string, along with the
buttons, shells, beads, sequins and any other sparkly things
you can find. Put each decorated string to one side.

3. Cut the fabric into strips roughly 1 m long by 15 cm wide.
Snip a small hole in the top end and thread a small piece of
string through the hole – this will be used to form a loop,
attaching the fabric strip to the longer piece of string.

4. Tie the long piece of string between two points
approximately a metre above the ground. Attach the strips of
fabric and the sparkly strings of charms to it.

THE SECRETS OF YOUR STAR SIGN

Your star sign, which depends on the date you were born, can reveal many secrets about you – your likes and dislikes and the sort of personality you have.

ARIES: 21 MARCH – 20 APRIL

You are competitive and want be a winner at everything you do. You have lots of energy, and use it to motivate your friends to do fun things.

Star Secret: You can be a bit bossy.

TAURUS: 21 APRIL – 21 MAY

You enjoy saving up your pocket money and spending it wisely. Bring on the bargains.

Star Secret: You can be stubborn.

GEMINI: 22 MAY – 21 JUNE

You love talking, so if you aren't gossiping with a friend, you're on the phone chatting away.

Star Secret: You tend to change your mind a lot.

CANCER: 22 JUNE – 22 JULY

Family and home are important to you. Nothing beats being with your mum and surrounded by the things in your room.

Star Secret: You can find it hard to tell people about your emotions and suffer from homesickness.

LEO: 23 JULY – 23 AUGUST

You are a serious Drama Queen. You probably have a special talent or hobby that gets you lots of attention, and your friends love to be around you.

Star Secret: You can be a bit of a show-off, and find it difficult when someone else is in the limelight.

VIRGO: 24 AUGUST – 22 SEPTEMBER

You like to feel healthy and eat your 'five-a-day' every day. You are a great organiser and rarely lose things.

Star Secret: You tend to be a bit critical of friends who are less organised than you are.

LIBRA: 23 SEPTEMBER – 23 OCTOBER

You are inseparable from your best friend, your 'partner in crime'. You are a peacemaker, and hate to watch people argue.

Star Secret: You get too involved in other people's problems and get upset quite easily.

SCORPIO: 24 OCTOBER – 22 NOVEMBER

This book was written for you, Miss Scorpio, because you love secrets and are excellent at keeping them. You know what you want in life.

Star Secret: You can come across as a bit scary when you really want something.

SAGITTARIUS: 23 NOVEMBER – 21 DECEMBER

You're interested in all life has to offer. You love new adventures, have a positive attitude and don't often get stressed.

Star Secret: You can be too busy thinking about what you want to think about others.

CAPRICORN: 22 DECEMBER – 20 JANUARY

You are a hard worker and love setting goals and achieving them. You enjoy helping your friends with their homework and enjoy explaining things to people.

Star Secret: You can be moody and tend to be too hard on yourself when you don't achieve a goal.

AQUARIUS: 21 JANUARY – 18 FEBRUARY

Your ideas are often different from those of the rest of your friends. You like to stand out from the crowd by wearing unusual outfits.

Star Secret: You're not good at sticking to the rules or being part of a team.

PISCES: 19 FEBRUARY – 20 MARCH

You have an uncanny ability to predict what the future holds. You like doing creative things too, such as drawing or writing.

Star Secret: You have been known to exaggerate the truth sometimes.

THE SECRET TO MAKING NEW FRIENDS

Have you ever wanted to introduce yourself to a group of new people but chickened out at the last minute? Making new friends can be scary. Here are some ways to ensure you make a great first impression, and even make friends for life.

Listen In. Before you approach a new group of people, listen in to what they are talking about. Prepare in your head something interesting to say about that subject. If, for example, they are talking about their favourite ball games, remember that new game you learnt to play on holiday. Now go over and tell them all about it – why not offer to show them how to play it?

Ask Questions. People like to be asked questions – it shows you are interested in them. Avoid asking questions that can be

answered only with a 'yes' or 'no', as this won't encourage them to chat. Instead of saying, 'So, you like horse riding then?' ask, 'What are your favourite things about horse riding?'

Offer Fun Ideas. People will be interested in becoming friends with you if they think you have new ideas for fun things to do. Suggest a sponsored skate at the local park, or find out who's up for forming a secret club (see pages 43–45).

Pay Compliments. Compliments are a great way to start off a conversation as they make people feel flattered. Why not tell someone you like their T-shirt, and ask them where they bought it from? Be sparing with your compliments, however – too many will make people think you aren't being honest.

Accept Invitations. If you are invited somewhere, say 'yes', even if it involves doing something you would not normally do. You are more likely to meet a new circle of people. For example, say 'yes' to a cinema trip even if it isn't a film you want to see.

HOW TO LEAVE A SECRET MESSAGE FOR THE FUTURE

Why not leave a box of secrets for someone to find years in the future? It's called a 'time capsule' and here's how make one.

You Will Need:

• a large jar, biscuit tin, or a plastic kitchen storage box – it must have a lid • masking tape • acrylic paint and brushes • a pen • some personal items for the future (see opposite page for ideas)

1. Decorate your capsule with flowers, stars or whatever you fancy. On the lid, use a permanent marker pen to write the words: *'Do not open until 2050'* (or whichever year you choose).

2. Leave your beautifully decorated capsule to dry completely.

3. Think carefully about what the items you place in your capsule say about you. What will they tell the person who discovers them in the future? Here are some ideas:

A newspaper headline showing what is happening in the world.

Photos of yourself and your friends.

Pictures from magazines of your favourite film and music stars.

Clippings from catalogues showing the type of clothes you love to wear.

A letter from you to the future – explain who you are and what your life is really like.

4. Shut the lid on your box of secrets and seal it using masking tape or strong glue.

HIDING YOUR BOX OF TREASURE

Hide your time capsule somewhere where it won't be discovered for many years. You could dig a hole in the flower bed or place it at the back of a seldom-used wardrobe. Why not ask your teacher if your class could make a time capsule to bury in the school grounds?

Warning. Always ask permission from your parents BEFORE you dig a hole in the middle their garden.

'X' MARKS THE SPOT

Once you have hidden your time capsule, you will need to make a map that shows any future time-capsule hunters (or your fifty-year-old self) exactly where to find it.

• Draw a rough sketch of your garden or house, as it would be viewed by someone looking down on it from above.

• Write out a 'key' down the side of the map to show landmarks that should still exist in the future, such as a big tree or a pond. If inside, show where windows and doorways are in a room. Draw a big 'X' to indicate where your time capsule is hidden.

• In case the landmarks you have marked disappear in the future, draw a compass in the corner of the map to indicate which direction is north in your map.

• Put your map in a safe place, away from prying eyes. For example, if you've buried your capsule in the garden, hide the map in the attic, tuck it behind your bed, or in the cupboard under the stairs.

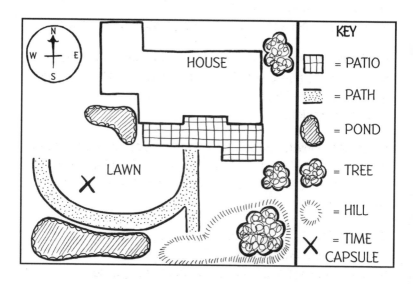

THE SECRET TO WINNING AN ARGUMENT

The secret to winning a battle of words is to stay calm, and follow the advice below.

Know Your Subject.
Bombarding your opponents with scientific facts is a sure-fire way to outwit them. If, for example, you want to eat chocolate for breakfast, explain that research has shown that chocolate increases levels of 'serotonin' – a substance that helps people feel happy. Convince your mum it's not such a bad idea on a Monday morning!

Get More Ammunition. If you feel that you are out of your depth, pretend you're popping off to use the loo. Quickly check your facts on the Internet, or phone a friend to get more ammunition.

Don't Back Down. Answer every single point put to you, even if it is only with, 'Yes, I understand, but I'm afraid I thoroughly disagree.' The other person will soon get so bored that she'll let you speak.

When All Else Fails. Start speaking calmly, almost in a whisper, then smile in a crazy manner. Your opponent will be so bamboozled she'll soon agree with anything you say.

THE SECRET TO A PERFECT NIGHT'S SLEEP

Follow this regime and discover the secret to a perfect night's sleep, filled with sweet dreams.

SLEEP SECRETS

• If you've been sitting down a lot during the day, take some light exercise about an hour before bedtime. Ask your mum or dad to go for a walk with you around the block, or do some star jumps in your bedroom.

• Avoid eating too close to bedtime, as your body will keep itself awake digesting the food. If you're hungry, eat a banana. These contain potassium – a chemical that helps you sleep.

• Next have a warm bath or shower. Don't make the water too hot, as it can have the effect of waking you up. A few drops of lavender or sandalwood oils in the water, will help you relax.

• Once you settle into bed, try to clear your head. If you are worried about forgetting something that you need to remember tomorrow, write it down before you try to sleep.

• Drink a mug of camomile tea or warm milk before you turn the lights out, to relax you.

• The temperature of your room should be quite cool, but your covers should be nice and cosy. If necessary, pop on an eye mask to shut out any light. Now you are ready to slip into a soothing, sweet slumber.

HOW TO PLAY THE SECRET TRAIL GAME

The Secret Trail Game is an excellent way to pass an afternoon in the open air with friends. Set a trail for your friends to follow and reward the most skillful pathfinder with a prize.

• Select a well-known landmark, such as the park gates or a fountain as the starting point for the trail. Indicate the direction in which your friends should start walking, by making a small pile of sticks or stones or leaves in the middle of the path they shouldn't take. Leave the correct path clear.

• If the path they are taking forks at any point, place a big stone with a smaller one on top where the path divides. Then place another small stone to the left or right of this, to indicate whether they take the left or right fork.

• Every twenty paces use sticks or stones to make an arrow shape on the ground to reassure your friends they are on the right path. Alternatively, use a piece of chalk to mark trees beside the path.

• Indicate the end of the trail, where the prize is hidden, with an 'X' of twigs or stones.

THE SECRET TO UNDERSTANDING YOUR FEELINGS

Learning to understand your emotions is an important part of growing up. The more you understand why you feel a certain way, the more comfortable you will be in your own skin. Do you recognise any of the confusing emotions described below? Find out what makes you feel this way and how to handle it.

Scenario One: Last week I hung out with my best friend the whole time, but this week she's hardly spoken to me, and spent all her time with another friend. I feel so mad at her!

Why Do I Feel This Way?: If a friend starts to ignore you and spends all her time with someone else, it may well make you feel jealous and hurt. Anger is also a natural reaction to feeling let down.

How To Handle It: Talk directly to your friend about her behaviour. Ask her if there is something wrong that you are unaware of. If she is still not very sympathetic and isn't worried about your feelings, then she may not have been such a good friend in the first place.

Scenario Two: I wish I looked like the cool girls in school. Even when I wear the same style clothes as they do, I still don't look as good. I just want to fit in.

Why Do I Feel This Way?: It is quite common to think that looking and acting like everybody else will make you popular and solve all your problems ... but you're wrong!

How To Handle It: Embrace your differences. Experiment with different fashions and stand out from the crowd. You could even wear T-shirts that say: 'Proud to be me!' Fitting in is not cool, it is just conforming. Being you is most definitely cool.

Scenario Three: I'm really good at acting and love being the centre of attention. Recently, however, I've noticed that people don't want to work in my group at drama club or be my acting partner. What's going on?

Why Do I Feel This Way?: If you are constantly trying to be in the limelight, it is possible others will eventually find this annoying and frustrating, and may stop wanting to work with you.

How To Handle It: It's great to be good at something and to have a special interest or talent, but don't forget to ensure other people in your group have the chance to participate, too. Everyone deserves their turn in the limelight, even those who are not as outgoing as you.

HOW TO MAKE COLOUR-CODED CAKES

Cakes are a great way to tell your friends what they mean to you. Ice your cakes with three colours from the colour chart on pages 26–27 to colour code them with secret meaning. This recipe makes nine cakes – perfect for a party or sleepover.

You Will Need:

• a rectangular cake tin • greaseproof paper • 2 mixing bowls, one large, one medium • wooden spoon • palette knife • wire rack • chopping board • three small bowls
For The Cake: • 250 g of butter • 250 g of caster sugar • 250 g of self-raising flour • 4 eggs
Colour-Coded Icing: • 100 g of butter • 200 g of icing sugar • 4 teaspoons of milk • three different colours of food colouring

MAKING THE CAKE

1. Preheat the oven to 180°C/ 350°F/ Gas Mark 4.

2. Line the bottom of the cake tin with greaseproof paper.

3. Soften the butter in a large saucepan or microwave.

4. Put all the cake ingredients into the large mixing bowl. Beat with the wooden spoon.

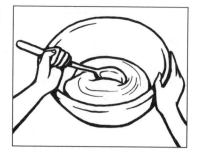

5. Pour the mixture into the tin, smoothing it down with the back of the spoon.

106

6. Pop in the oven for 30 minutes or until your cake is golden brown and has risen.

Warning. Always wear oven gloves and get an adult to help you when using an oven.

7. Remove your cake from the oven, and leave to cool.

8. Loosen the edges of the cake with a palette knife, and turn out on to the wire rack to cool completely. When it has cooled down, peel off the greaseproof paper.

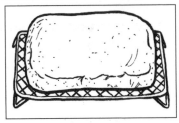

COLOUR-CODED ICING

9. To make your icing, beat the butter, icing sugar and milk together in the medium-sized mixing bowl until it forms a smooth paste. Add a few drops of water if necessary to make it easier to spread.

10. Divide this mixture into the three small bowls. Add one shade of food colouring to each bowl.

11. Place the cake on the chopping board and cut into three parts. Ice each of these parts using a different colour icing.

12. Cut each section of the iced cakes into a further three pieces.

Now you can select which colour cake should be given to which friend – the colour you give will let them know how you feel about them. Here are a few suggestions:

Blue icing means you make me feel calm and relaxed. I feel I can be myself around you.
Red icing means you are my best friend and I can tell you anything.
Yellow icing means you make me laugh out loud! When I am with you, I am always happy.

THE SECRET TO SURVIVING A SCHOOL BULLY

Anyone who puts you down, makes jokes at your expense, shouts insults at you or spreads lies about you, is a bully. As soon as you realise someone is bullying you, you need to act.

DON'T STOOP TO THEIR LEVEL

If you are being victimised, it may be tempting to look for an opportunity to get the bully back, to humiliate them in public. However, this may only make the problem worse. Walk away from someone whose behaviour is aggressive or threatening. Head to somewhere where there are lots of other people, where you are safe. Never resort to physical violence yourself.

TAKE ACTION IMMEDIATELY

A bully is a coward who will only pick on someone she thinks is unable to stand up to her. Prove her wrong by taking action. Write down exactly what has been said and done to you, so you have an accurate record of the bully's actions. Then tell an adult exactly what has happened. Ask for advice on how to deal with the specific situation you find yourself in. There is no shame in getting help from an adult. It is a brave decision to take.

ACT BRAVE

The best action you can take is to ignore the person who is tormenting you and get on with your life. If a bully thinks that she is no longer able to upset you, she will soon get bored and leave you alone.

HOW TO PLAY A SECRET TRICK

Here are two cool tricks to play on your friends and family. It is essential that you never give away the secret of how they work.

LOOK NO HANDS

Pop an ice cube into a glass of water. Challenge your friend to pick the ice cube out of the glass without touching it and give her just a length of thread and some salt to help her. She will fail to manage.

Now it is your turn. Simply lay the piece of thread across the middle of the ice cube. Sprinkle about a teaspoon of salt over the top. After one minute, the thread will stick to the ice cube. Now take hold of one end of the thread and lift the ice cube out of the glass.

SNATCH AND GRAB

Mix together 500 g of cornflour and 100 ml of water in a large bowl. Drop a pound coin into the bottom of the bowl. Challenge your friend to find the coin in less than a minute. If she manages, she can keep the coin.

She will hurriedly grapple around in the bowl, but will find she is unable to move her hand quickly enough in the mixture to find the coin in time. This is because rapid movement causes this magic mix to turn solid.

When it is your turn, put your hand in the mixture and move it around slowly, searching until you find and pull out the coin.

HOW TO TELL IF SOMEONE IS LYING

If you suspect someone isn't telling you the truth, there are some tricks you can use to catch them out. Carry out these secret tests and work out if you are being told the truth.

TEST ONE. Change the subject completely. If your friend seems visibly relieved, she may be hiding something.

TEST TWO. Liars often smile more than usual to throw you off the scent – but is her smile a fake? Real smiles reach the eyes, so the skin around the eyes may crinkle and the eyes narrow a little. A fake smile uses only the mouth.

TEST THREE. If you suspect that your friend is lying, don't question her directly, simply encourage her to talk freely. The more she talks, the more her story is likely to come unravelled, and the truth will emerge.

TEST FOUR. Bringing the hand to the face – touching the nose or stroking the chin – are all movements that liars make. Someone who is lying may make more eye contact than normal as a way of making you think they are being honest.

TEST FIVE. Consider how your friend acts normally. If she is more jumpy than usual or makes excuses to leave, she may not have told you the truth about something.

Warning. Never accuse someone of lying if you are not absolutely convinced she is – you will only upset her and lose her trust as a friend.

THE SECRET TO COPING WITH EMBARRASSMENT

When something embarrassing happens, every girl should have a secret strategy to ensure she keeps her cool.

What If ... Someone Is Wearing The Same Dress As You? Smile and make a joke of it. March up to the other girl and say, 'Hey, looks like we've both got the best taste at this party!'

What If ... Your Skirt Is Tucked Into Your Knickers? Don't panic – hardly anyone will have noticed. If they have, just smile, shrug and change the subject. If people can see you aren't bothered, they won't find it entertaining to tease you.

What If ... You Put Your Foot In It? Blame your own ignorance for your comment. For example, if you said, 'I really hate cats,' and someone says, 'But I have cats!', say 'Sorry, I just don't know anything about them. I'm sure if I met your cats I'd love them!' She'll be impressed by your interest and forget your mistake.

THE SECRET TO MAKING PEOPLE FEEL COMFORTABLE

If people feel relaxed around you, they'll enjoy your company and want to be around you more. Here are the secrets to making others feel instantly at ease.

Be Sensitive. If a friend seems down and isn't saying much, she probably isn't in the mood for messing around and being silly. Ask her if she'd like to talk about what's on her mind. If she says no, suggest watching a funny movie together instead – this should help her to relax.

Practise Open Body Language. Use 'friendly' forms of body language to make other people feel comfortable. For example, showing them the palms of your hands indicates that you are being honest. Copying their hand movements will reassure them that you like them. See page 66-67 for more tips on how to use body language to transmit secret signals.

Use Body Contact. Occasionally touching someone lightly on the arm, shoulder or hand when you are speaking to them, will help them feel at ease.

Use People's Names. People feel that you are interested in them or care about them if you use their name at the end of a sentence. It shows that you are talking to them in a very direct and personal way. Be careful not to do it too much though – it can start to sound odd!

HOW TO MAKE A SECRET POCKET

A secret pocket is great for hiding anything, from secret messages to the key to your codes, or simply for storing your lunch money. Make the secret pocket described below and keep a secret item on you at all times.

You Will Need:

• a pair of socks • an old, holey sock in the same colour as your good socks • thread in the same colour as your socks • a needle • pins • dressmaking scissors • a ruler

1. Take one of the good socks and lay it flat on the floor. Measure the width of the top of the sock.

2. Cut out a piece of the old sock, the same length as the width of your sock and 5 cm high.

3. Turn the sock inside out and lay it flat on the floor again.

4. Pin the piece of fabric from the old sock against the good sock, making sure that the pins do not go through to the other side of the sock.

5. Using the needle and thread, stitch along the bottom end of the fabric and up along the two sides. Leave the top side open – this is the opening of the pocket.

Be careful not to go all the way through to the other side of the sock and accidentally sew both sides of the sock together.

Top Tip. Make sure your stitches are quite small and close together – this will ensure that nothing will be able to fall out of the pocket as you walk around.

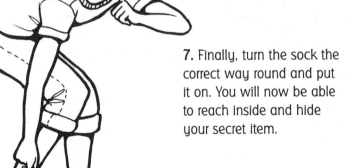

6. When you have finished sewing the fabric to the sock, tie a double knot in the end of the thread to make sure that it won't unravel when you wear it.

7. Finally, turn the sock the correct way round and put it on. You will now be able to reach inside and hide your secret item.

HOW TO PLAY THE SPIN-A-SECRET GAME

The Spin-A-Secret Game is a great way to get to know your friends better and find out their best-kept secrets. Be prepared, however, to spill the beans yourself …

You Will Need:

- three players or more • an empty, clean glass bottle
  - a pen and a few pieces of paper for each player

HOW TO PLAY

1. Sit in a circle with your friends and lay the bottle on its side in the middle of the circle on the floor.

2. One of you must spin the bottle first.

3. The person to whom the neck of the bottle points when the bottle stops spinning is the 'Confessor'. She must 'confess' three 'secrets' – only one of which is true. She then writes the true secret on a piece of paper, but keeps it hidden from the other players.

For example, she might say:

'I once forgot to put my shoes on and went to school in my slippers.'
'My parents named me "Gertrude" but I changed my name before I started school.'
'I once fed my dog ice cream and it made him sick.'

4. Now it is the turn of the group to guess which secret is true. They can discuss their suspicions together, but they must agree on just one of the secrets. If they do not guess correctly, the Confessor does not have to reveal which was the true secret. However, if the group does guess the secret correctly, the Confessor must unfold the piece of paper to verify their choice. The group can then ask the Confessor to choose between telling the group another true secret or doing a forfeit. Here are some excellent forfeits you can get her to perform.

Put all her clothes on backwards, then walk around the block for five minutes.
Do a silly hairstyle and wear it for the rest of the night.
Don't speak at all for the next ten minutes.

5. After the Confessor has revealed a new secret or performed a forfeit, she spins the bottle to select a new Confessor.

HOW TO PERFORM MIND-READING TRICKS

Impress your friends with these cool mind-reading tricks and watch them marvel at your powers. You don't have to be psychic to read someone's mind – just never reveal the secret of how you did it.

NAME DROP

Gather your friends. Ask each of them to think of a famous person. Then ask one of them to call out the name they thought of. Say, for example, she says 'David Beckham'. Write his name down on a slip of paper and drop it into a hat.

Now ask each person in turn to call out the name of the famous person who they were thinking of. Pretend to write down each name on a separate slip of paper and pop it in the hat. However, instead of writing different names, just write the original name (in this case David Beckham) each time.

Now ask one of your friends to pick a piece of paper from the hat. Tell her not to tell you what name is written on it.

Hold your head and appear to think deeply. Tell your friends that you can predict what name is on the paper she has in her hand. Write down the original name (David Beckham) on a large piece of card and hold it up to the group, so everybody can see it. Ask your friend to show the group the name she has on the paper she pulled out from the hat. Watch the amazement spread across your friends' faces as they discover you are correct.

Don't repeat the trick and make sure you destroy all the slips of paper after your performance
to keep your trick secret.

PREDICTIVE POINTING

For your next trick you will need an assistant who knows the trick you are about to perform. Gather your friends in your bedroom again. Tell them that you will step outside while they choose any object in the room. You will then come back into the room and tell them what object they selected.

Leave the room and return when summoned. Your assistant then points to different objects in the room, asking whether they were the ones chosen. You will amaze your audience by knowing which object they chose.

The secret behind this trick is simple. Immediately before pointing to the chosen object, your assistant must point to an object in the room that has LEGS – a chair, a table or a person. You will know that the next object pointed to is the chosen one.

HOW TO PLAN A SURPRISE PARTY

Organising a surprise birthday party for a friend is rewarding just for the look on her face when she realises what is happening. Here's how to plan the perfect party and ensure your surprise comes off without a hitch.

COUNTDOWN TO PARTY TIME

Four Weeks To Go. Decide on a theme for your party, such as 'Under the Sea', or 'Secret Safari'. Alternatively, ask everyone to dress as something beginning with the first letter of your friend's name. If her name is Philippa, it's a 'P party' – pirates, princesses, policewomen, penguins and painters, for example.

Send out your invitations, but don't forget to write in big letters that this is a SURPRISE party!

Get the birthday girl's parents in on the act – ask them to tell her that they are taking her out on the evening of her birthday. She won't suspect a thing.

Two Weeks To Go. Plan the music. Make a playlist on your computer or MP3 player. Put together music that suits the party's theme – for example, for a nineties party include lots of cheesy nineties hits.

Collect together a selection of photos of the birthday girl – her parents might be able to help you with this. Print them out big or enlarge them using a photocopier.

The Day Before. Organise your party food – again taking any theme you have chosen into account. If it is a 'yellow party', why not feature crisps, corn on the cob, pineapple rings, lemon cake, lemonade and banana milkshakes?

The Big Day. Decorate the party room. Put up the blown-up photos of your friend on the walls using sticky tack. For an 'Under the Sea' theme, replace the light bulb with a blue one to give the room an underwater effect – ask an adult to help with this. Hang blue and green sheets from the walls, and put lots of shells on all the tables and shelves. You could even fill up the bath with water and put some plastic fish in there.

One Hour To Go. The birthday girl will be getting ready to go on her 'birthday treat'. Arrange for her parents to bring her to your house at a specific time, supposedly to pick you up to come with her on the treat. Gather your guests in the party room and turn the lights off. When your friend knocks, open the door and pretend you have forgotten something. Ask her to come inside while you get it. Lead her to the party room, turn on the light and ... one, two, three ... 'Surprise!'

HOW TO CUSTOMISE CLASSIC CODES

In the past, men and women were not permitted to talk to each other openly in public. Instead, secret codes were invented specifically to allow them to exchange messages.

Here is a modern version of a classic code that you can use to communicate secretly with your crush – and one you can use to communicate with your best mates.

LANGUAGE OF FLOWERS

Traditionally, the gift of certain flowers carry very specific meanings. Consult the up-dated list below and send your crush the secret message of your choice.

- A single rose bud is the symbol of true love.

- A bunch of hand-picked buttercups means 'You cheer me up when I am down.'

- A pink carnation means 'I will never forget you.'

- Ivy shows you will stay loyal to them.

- A yellow rose means you are feeling jealous.

- Sunflowers mean 'I hope that all your wishes will come true.'

- And everyone knows that at Christmas a branch of mistletoe with its white berries means 'Give me a kiss, please!'

THE LANGUAGE OF THE FAN

In Victorian times, ladies didn't just use their pretty hand-held fans to cool themselves down – by positioning their fans in different ways, they used them to send secret messages.

Adopt this latter-day language of fans using your pen instead. Here are a few pen flutterings you could try:

• Spinning the pen quickly around in your fingers in front of your face means 'My big crush has just walked in the room.'

• Stroking your chin with the pen means 'I don't really fancy him any more.'

• Tapping the end of your pen against the palm of your hand means 'Find an excuse to leave the room, I need to talk to you now.'

• Tapping your pen on the desk means 'Watch out, you are spilling all your secrets and it's time to stop.'

Make up some more of your own and agree on them with your friends.

HOW TO COPE WITH A SECRET CRUSH

If you've ever had a secret crush, you'll know it's hard to stay calm when he's around. Luckily, there are a few secrets to keeping in control, even when your stomach is doing back flips.

IF YOUR CRUSH ...

Ignores You. Don't Panic. This may not mean he doesn't like you. He may be shy or just bad at talking to girls! Maybe your crush likes you, and is trying to disguise it by being cold. Don't spend your time moping about it. Instead, keep busy, and have fun with your own friends – they'll soon wish they were joining in with you.

Makes Fun Of You. Being unkind could be a way of disguising their own crush – on you. Why else would they pay you so much attention? However, if they're just being cruel for the sake of it then they're not worth having a crush on. Move on to liking someone else – there are plenty more fish in the sea!

Talks To Lots Of Other Girls. If your crush has lots of girls as friends, don't be jealous. Try to be calm about it and act like you don't care. If your crush has a crush on you too, they might well try and make an excuse for you both to hang out alone together.

Asks To Walk Home From School With You. Don't panic, this is a good sign. Try to relax and act as if they are one of your friends. Be yourself and chat away like you would with your best friend.

HOW TO MAKE A CARD FOR YOUR SECRET VALENTINE

If you have a secret crush on someone, why not make them a card for Valentine's Day with a message inside that is for their eyes only?

You Will Need:

• A4 piece of pink card • ruler • scissors • a piece of red fabric at least 15 cm by 11 cm • PVA glue • pen or pencil

1. Fold the card in half. Cut along the crease to divide the card into two.

2. Take one of the pieces of card and fold it in half again. Cut this piece into two.

3. Dot some glue all over one side of one of the smaller pieces of card.

4. Carefully glue the red fabric to the front of this piece of card and smooth it down.

5. Turn this piece of card over and draw a heart shape that takes up most of the space, as shown.

6. Once dry, cut around the outline of the heart so you have a heart-shaped, fabric-covered piece of card.

7. Take the larger piece of card and fold it in two (use the ruler to make a nice sharp crease). This will make the base of your Valentine's card.

8. Turn your red heart over so that the fabric side is face down. Glue around the outer edges of the heart, stopping as you reach the two curves at the top. Make sure that the two curves at the top do not have any glue on them.

9. Turn the heart over and press it down carefully onto the front of your Valentine's card. Leave to dry completely.

10. When the glue is dry, pop a clue to your identity inside the pocket that you have made in the top part of the heart – a photo of yourself, or a secret message. How much detail you include will depend on how easily you want your crush to guess who their secret Valentine is ...

THE SECRET TO DOING WELL AT SCHOOL

Smart girls know there is a secret to doing well at school. Follow these simple dos and don'ts and prepare to be top of the class by next month.

DO eat foods that boost your brainpower – these include fish, eggs, salad, yogurt and beans. Eat porridge or cereal for breakfast to give your brain the energy it needs to think clearly.

DON'T do your homework in front of the TV. Try to find a quiet place to do it so that you can concentrate. Always do your homework as soon as you get home from school – what you have learnt in the day will still be fresh in your mind.

DO your research. If you are interested in a particular topic, do some research in your own time. For example, if you are interested in outer space, visit the library and look for books on astronomy, and cut things out from the newspapers that teach you facts about the planets.

DON'T pack your schoolbag in the morning – you are bound to forget something you need. Instead, the night before, get everything ready that you will need for the next day. Being organised will start your day off well – and will mean that you get to school in plenty of time, calm and ready to learn.

DO ask friends and family to test you on what you have learnt. This will help you to remember the information more easily and highlight the bits you don't understand.

ALSO AVAILABLE:

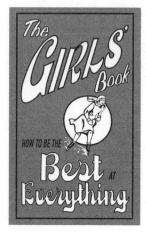

The Girls' Book: How To
Be The Best At Everything
ISBN: 978-1-905158-79-9

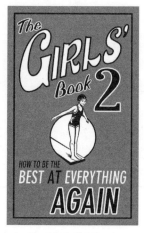

The Girls' Book 2: How To
Be The Best At Everything Again
ISBN: 978-1-906082-32-1

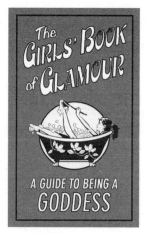

The Girls' Book Of Glamour
A Guide To Being A Goddess
ISBN: 978-1-906082-13-0

Coming soon:

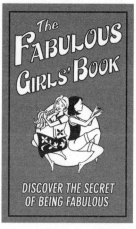

The Fabulous Girls' Book
Discover The Secret Of Being Fabulous
ISBN: 978-1-906082-52-9